Boomers in Paradise
Living in Puerto Vallarta

by Robert Nelson

D1018141

Copyright © 2008 Robert Nelson
All rights reserved.

ISBN: 1-4392-0686-4
ISBN-13: 9781439206867

Visit www.booksurge.com to order additional copies.

FOR JAN

CONTENTS

Introduction

In 2001, my wife and I purchased a retirement home in Mismaloya, a few miles south of Puerto Vallarta, Mexico, and planned a move to our tropical paradise a few years later. Troubles in the technology sector shortly after we purchased the home, though, negatively affected my brand consulting business, so we accelerated our plan to move to Mexico. We sold our home in Morgan Hill, California, gave away most of our furniture, and moved south of the border lock, stock, and barrel.

As we eased ourselves into the local stream of expats, we noticed that many were younger than us, mostly baby boomers, part of the over seventy-eight million strong bubble born between 1946 and 1964. Jan and I, born in 1943, were considered the older siblings of the baby boomer generation. Although we moved to Vallarta when we were fifty-nine, I was not yet retired. I continued operating my consulting business from my home in Mismaloya, servicing several U.S.-based clients. As we began to know more people, we could see a major lifestyle trend emerging: baby boomers were not waiting for retirement to enjoy paradise. As always, the highly independent, adventurous boomers wanted what they wanted, now.

For most boomers, retirement means something completely different from the generations that have gone before them. The old retirement model doesn't work for restless baby boomers. Vallarta boomers—almost all are under sixty—couldn't wait for retirement to enjoy their paradise and landed on our shores before they reached retirement age, seeking adventure and new life experiences.

This book profiles a wide slice of local baby boomers who represent the path-breaking characteristics of their boomer brethren in the United States and Canada. Several common threads are woven through their stories. First and foremost is their sense of adventure. A few came to Mexico many years ago when they were very young, speak Spanish fluently, and have integrated themselves completely into the local culture. Most fell in love with Vallarta while on vacation and made an emotional commitment to live in paradise now, not later. All wanted a unique lifestyle and weren't willing to settle for the ordinary.

Living in Vallarta has meant working for most, usually in the real estate industry or owning small businesses. In keeping with their generation's view of life and retirement, Vallarta boomers plan to keep working well beyond traditional retirement age. The old retirement model is not for them.

For the majority of PV baby boomers, the tropical magic of Vallarta's paradise has not worn off, but a few have adjusted their rose-colored glasses and see the city through a more pragmatic prism. All have had some frustrations with living in PV. They discovered, though, that how you handle those frustrations ultimately determines your level of comfort with everyday living here.

This book was written for baby boomers everywhere who may be thinking of a life adventure south of the border and may be considering Puerto Vallarta for retirement, for work, or for both. The best way to learn about a place, I think, is to get to know the people who live there. In this book, you'll find out about what it's like to live in Puerto Vallarta through the lives and experiences of fourteen boomers and near-boomers, some of them well-regarded experts on media, law, real estate, and health care. The book's first chapter provides an overview of key baby boomer trends, including the rising migration to Mexico and Puerto Vallarta. The last chapter features personal interviews with the directors of tourism for both the city of

Puerto Vallarta and the state of Jalisco. These two local experts provide an authoritative view of what the future holds for Puerto Vallarta and the surrounding area, an important consideration for anyone contemplating relocating to this fast-growing, international resort city.

Most importantly, you'll find both the good and the bad about PV in this book. This is not a book approved by the local chamber of commerce, but an honest view of what it is like to live in Puerto Vallarta, based upon many hours of personal interviews I conducted with the boomers you will meet in these pages. If you are thinking about joining us in paradise, this book's for you.

CHAPTER ONE

BOOMERS SEEKING PARADISE

The "giant sucking sound" that presidential candidate Ross Perot talked about during the 1992 U.S. election campaign is no longer just about American jobs heading south as a result of the NAFTA treaty. It's now more about the increasing numbers of American and Canadian baby boomers chasing the sun to Mexico for vacation homes, retirement, or just for a new life adventure as they seek their vision of paradise.

The full strength of the boomer wave will soon hit the shores of Mexico as the oldest of the more than seventy-eight–million–person cohort turns sixty-two this year and becomes eligible for Social Security. Another nearly ten million Canadian baby boomers soon will join their American counterparts on the march south. A product of the postwar economic expansion, baby boomers started arriving on the scene in 1946. The boomer baby bubble finally burst in 1964 with the widespread use of the birth control pill, but not before the wave swamped schools and other institutions in its path.

Over the next two decades, this single largest demographic group in the history of the United States will reach retirement age after impacting virtually every aspect of American life and culture. And in line with their lifetime societal influence, baby boomers are poised to profoundly change the way Americans retire.

The leading edge of the wave in the United States—over three million boomers—turns sixty-two in 2008 and will be facing lifestyle and retirement choices that certainly will be influenced by how much money they have accumulated. A MetLife Mature Market Institute study from 2007—entitled "Boomers: Ready to Launch"—profiles baby boomers born in the year 1946 and finds that the oldest boomers have an annual income of $71,400, a net worth—excluding home value—of $257,800, a home valued at $297,900, and have received or expect to receive some inheritance from their parents in a range of $113,000 to $210,000.

Although these older boomers have acquired substantial assets, baby boomers in general feel they need more money for retirement. An earlier MetLife study conducted in 2005—"The MetLife Survey of American Attitudes Toward Retirement"—finds that boomers are increasingly likely to delay retirement until they believe they have enough money to retire. Over half of baby boomers expect to continue working well past initial retirement age because of economic pressures to maintain their income. But, nearly 70 percent of those who plan to keep working say they just have a desire to remain active and engaged during retirement. Many boomers will be working longer primarily because they want to work.

The MetLife study is reinforced by new research in 2007 conducted by the Society of Actuaries, a professional organization based in Schaumburg, Illinois. That organization found that 63 percent of respondents near retirement age are concerned that the value of their savings won't keep up with inflation. Further, of those surveyed who were still working, 15 percent say they expect to work past sixty-five and 28 percent say they don't expect to retire at all. That number, however, also includes both people who want to work and those who think they will have to because they will need the money. The pre-retirement group surveyed—baby boomers between forty-five and sixty-two—is generally more worried about finances than those who have already stopped working.

Additional research by Civic Ventures—a San Francisco-based aging issues think tank—supports the boomer trend to continue to work in retirement. Their study finds that four out of five people over fifty would like to continue to work either part-time or full-time during retirement. Miriam Goodman—the author of *Reinventing Retirement: 389 Bright Ideas about Family, Friends, Health, What to Do and Where to Live*—adds: "Unlike our parents, for the baby boomer generation, retirement is more than 'not working.' We are younger, healthier, and better educated then any generation before. We're not exhausted by years of heavy labor. We have twenty or thirty active, productive years ahead of us, and we need help figuring out what to do with that time."

Puerto Vallarta-based retirement coach Dee Dee Camhi agrees. "People entering the third phase of their lives are quite different from their parents and grandparents. Boomers have health, more money, more mobility, and more time. Many shifts have occurred in Western society allowing individuals to think about retirement in a totally different way. The word retirement in English means 'to retire from.' In Spanish, the word for retirement is jubilación, which means celebration. Maybe that is why we see so many baby boomers in Mexico celebrating their lives as opposed to retiring from them."

Boomers are once again redefining the age in which they live. The baby boomer take on retirement is playing out south of the border in ways few could have anticipated. Fueled by abundant sunshine, lower living costs, good quality health care, and proximity to the U.S. and Canada, baby boomer adventurers are heading to Mexico in ever-increasing numbers to buy second homes, retire, work, and just to play. The Mexican

Association of Real Estate Professionals estimates that nearly one and a half million Americans own homes in Mexico. The association also predicts that number could climb to twelve million by 2025, driven primarily by the swell of baby boomers. Confirming this trend, the American Association of Retired Professionals ranks Mexico number four among places in the world Americans are moving to retire.

The rush to foreign lands is being led by the baby boomer generation. The director-general of Mexico's tourism development agency, FONATUR, profiles the typical investor in Mexico real estate as American and Canadian baby boomers who have paid off most of their initial home mortgage and are coming into inheritance money. Boomers are increasingly snapping up Mexican resort properties for use as primary residences for both full-time retirement and work or second homes for part-time retirement or vacation.

Although anecdotal projections of Americans living in Mexico often exceed one million, the U.S. State Department projection shows more than five-hundred thousand Americans living throughout the country, but they acknowledge that is a low number. In fact, the U.S.-based National Law Center—a Tucson, Arizona research institute—claims that U.S. and Canadian property ownership in Mexico more than doubled in the past decade in the most popular areas and is growing at more than 10 percent a year. They said Americans and Canadians account for about 90 percent of foreign ownership.

Mexico's baby boomer attraction is underscored by the country's number one ranking in 2007 by *International Living* magazine as the world's most popular retirement destination. Over a fifteen-year period, the publication has developed what it calls the Annual Global Retirement Index, which was designed to help those who are contemplating retirement better evaluate and compare popular international retirement areas.

The Annual Global Retirement Index is based on eight weighted criteria developed by the magazine:

- Cost of Living—20 percent

- Health Care—20 percent

- Special Benefits—20 percent

- Real Estate—15 percent

- Entertainment, Recreation, and Culture—10 percent

- Climate—5 percent

- Safety and Stability—5 percent

- Infrastructure—5 percent

The 2007 Annual Global Retirement Index places Mexico at the top as the number one country in the world for retirement, displacing perennial favorite Panama. *International Living* reports: "Mexico offers the perfect mix of centuries-old traditions and contemporary lifestyles. Moving to Mexico means you can still have all of the amenities you grew accustomed to north of the border: cable TV, high-speed Internet, and modern home appliances. And if you prefer, when you move to Mexico, you can even bring all of your favorite things with you without paying import taxes. Goods and services cost less, so you can afford the kinds of luxuries only the very wealthy enjoy up north: a maid, a cook, and a gardener, for example. In your retirement here, you'll have time to volunteer at the local school, time to golf in the mornings, time to relax on the beach, time to savor life."

International Living further points out that Mexico is a very diverse country where retirees can choose between water, mountains, or both, and, because of the country's geographic diversity, retirees can pick their climate: hot and dry in northern Mexico, hot and humid in the south and the coastal areas, and year-round spring in Mexico's Colonial Highlands.

For real estate, the publication gives Mexico a score of 84 percent, citing the "endless possibilities" and remarks: "Despite what you may have heard, it's not too late to buy real estate here."

Mexico is a large country with many retirement living choices. *International Living* recommends eleven areas within the country that it believes make the most sense for expatriate living, based on their Annual Global Retirement Index criteria: Rosarito Beach, Puerto Vallarta, San Miguel de Allende, Queretaro, Mazatlan, Merida, La Paz, Campeche, Playa del Carmen/Riviera Maya, Ajijic/Chapala, and Sayulita/San Francisco.

By any gauge, Puerto Vallarta has become one of the top spots in the country for American and Canadian retirees, second home owners, and baby boomer adventurers. Anecdotally, Vallarta's expatriate community is said to number over twenty thousand full-time and part-time residents, second only to the Lake Chapala/Ajijic area, south of Guadalajara, a long-time retirement haven for winter-weary Americans and Canadians. Mexico's National Immigration Institute (INM) reported in 2007 that over fifty-six thousand foreign-born residents call the state of Jalisco home, which encompasses both Puerto Vallarta and the Lake Chapala area. Approximately half are Americans and Canadians. That number understates the actual number of expats, however, because it only includes those with visas who live in Mexico over six months each year and doesn't capture those with just tourist cards who live in Mexico part-time.

Over the past 157 years, Puerto Vallarta has grown from a tiny fishing village on the eastern shore of the Bay of Banderas to a modern city of well over 350,000. Located on the same latitude as Hawaii, the "Jewel of the Mexican Riviera," is blessed with a similar climate and topography.

Puerto Vallarta gained international fame when U.S. film director John Huston shot Tennessee Williams' *The Night of the Iguana* at Mismaloya beach in 1963. The publicity surrounding the making of the film and the off-camera romance between Richard Burton and Elizabeth Taylor piqued the interest of international travelers seeking a new tropical "in spot."

The romance continues today as Puerto Vallarta welcomes over two million American and Canadian visitors each year and has become the favored tropical resort destination of thousands of American and Canadian retirees, second home owners, and adventurous baby boomers.

Just how many boomers seek their little slice of paradise each year? Vallarta Lifestyles Group publisher and editor-in-chief John Youden keeps track of real estate trends in Puerto Vallarta and what he calls Costa Vallarta, which encompasses the Bay of Banderas as well as the northern Pacific shore of the neighboring state of Nayarit.

"In 2000 Puerto Vallarta had roughly fifty million dollars in resort real estate sales ('resort real estate' is defined as real estate purchased primarily by retirees or second home purchasers)," Youden reports. "There were rarely homes selling for more than one million dollars and few large real estate developers. In 2007 there was more than five hundred million dollars in resort real estate sales, with condos selling for over two million dollars and homes in excess of five million dollars. There were more than one hundred developments spread out around Banderas Bay, allowing Puerto Vallarta to lead in sales volume for resort real estate in Mexico, ahead of major markets such as Los Cabos, Acapulco, and Cancun."

Youden ticks off the current projects in the local real estate development pipeline: "Today, there are five mega-developments, with more than one hundred projects under construction. There are seven golf courses, with three more in the planning or development stage. There are three marinas, with more boat slips than anywhere else in Mexico. And, Vallarta—or Costa Vallarta as the region is now known—continues to offer myriad real estate options and price points. Although there are million-dollar homes and condos available up and down the coast, there are still properties available for around a hundred thousand dollars—you just won't be on the beach."

For those baby boomers ready and primed to pick up their piece of paradise, John Youden believes that Puerto Vallarta has many advantages over the other resort destinations in Mexico, particularly the areas recommended by *International Living* magazine. "An important advantage is the foothills of the Sierra Madres that surround the bay. They have allowed homes on the hillsides to be nearly as valuable as beach front because of their views of the bay. This is something Cancun, and Los Cabos to a certain extent, can't provide. Puerto Vallarta also has the downtown central area, which has retained its charm and character. There is the Malecon boardwalk, unique to the town, along with a river running through the middle of town, creating the Cuale Island—the town's 'Central Park.' To the south, it is rich in tropical foliage, whereas to the north it becomes semi-arid. There are numerous rivers flowing into beautiful Banderas Bay, a bay perfect for boating, offering wind for sailors nearly every day of the year. Vallarta is close to major markets in the U.S. and has excellent airlift from major airlines servicing the region. Although there was no major plan established for the destination, all the pieces necessary to create a successful resort real estate destination were in place when the demand built up in 2003."

The run-up in real estate values in the U.S. and Canada coincided with the escalation in Puerto Vallarta housing demand that began in 2003. Availability of low interest equity loans north of the border also helped propel the surging local housing market, along with the new option of reasonable home financing terms through a wide range of lenders.

As baby boomers begin to close in on their version of retirement, even more will be looking south to seek their vision of paradise, following the sun and the leading-edge boomer adventurers who already call Puerto Vallarta home. This book tells the tales of those adventurers who have paved the path to paradise for those who have yet to follow.

CHAPTER TWO

MARIA O'CONNOR

Single
Chicago, Illinois
Attorney, Tropicasa Real Estate

"Don't leave your brain at the border and come down
here and think things are done that differently. They're
not, especially when you're buying property."

At forty-four, Maria O'Connor represents the tail end of the
baby boomer generation. She was born and raised in Chicago,
as were her mom and dad. Her family moved to the northern
suburb of Evanston when she was about three, and then farther
north to Glencoe when she turned seven. Maria has two younger
brothers, an investment banker father, and a concert violinist
and schoolteacher mom, who influenced her to attend the University of Illinois at Champaign/Urbana, where she majored in
history and minored in political science. Following graduation
she moved back to Chicago and got a job with a law firm as a
law clerk and paralegal and also attended law school at night.
After graduating from law school in 1990, she took some time
off to find out what she wanted to do with her life. "I really
hated Chicago weather, and, as trite as that sounds, it was the
impetus for my relocation to PV," Maria explains.

Maria saw Puerto Vallarta for the first time as an undergraduate in 1985. She had been to Cancun and was planning a new trip there when a terrible hurricane made her change her plans. Her travel agent helpfully recommended Puerto Vallarta. The only thing she knew about Vallarta, though, was what she remembered from the old television series *The Love Boat*. She liked Cancun a lot because of its beaches, but when she arrived here she was absolutely floored. "When I saw the mountains and the jungle for the first time, it was amazing. I stayed at the Playa de Oro, which was close to where the cruise ships came in. I was so intrigued that there were no televisions or telephones in any of the hotel rooms. I liked that very much. I would get my cup of coffee in the morning and walk over to the cruise ship area to hear the mariachis playing at seven in the morning as the ships would dock, and then finish my coffee and go lie on the beach all day. What a great introduction to PV."

After returning to Chicago, she told all of her friends about Vallarta because she had fallen hopelessly in love with its beauty, and it was just a hop, skip, and a jump from Chicago. "You could get on a Mexicana flight at nine in the morning and be here by noon," Maria remembers. "We would fly down on Friday and go home on Monday. It was a perfect long weekend. I came to Vallarta eleven times between 1985 and 1990 before I finally moved here. I mostly came for long weekends because I was working at the law firm and going to school at night."

The longest time Maria spent in PV before she moved here full-time was three weeks. She was supposed to go with a friend, but her friend had to cancel, so she came by herself. She was surprised to find so many people traveling by themselves, which she found she liked. "I loved traveling alone. I didn't have to worry about anything. I could go where I wanted, when I wanted. I still love traveling by myself," she says.

With each trip to PV, she would inch closer to town until finally she started staying at the Playa Los Arcos on the south side of the Cuale River. "At that time many of the roads past the Tropicana hotel were made of dirt, which caused problems when it rained, but I didn't care a bit," she laughs. "It just added to the laid-back atmosphere of the town."

Maria has been a world traveler for many years and has seen many beautiful places, but she puffs up with pride when she speaks of her adopted city. "I tell people that there are beautiful places all over the world, but none more beautiful than Puerto Vallarta. I've traveled throughout Europe and even lived for a few months in Italy. In fact, two years after I moved to Vallarta I went to Rome for three months thinking it might be an even better place to live. It wasn't. I came back to Vallarta for one important reason: the people. The people who live in this city are the nicest people I've ever met. They are so proud of their country and their city. I've found that when people say they've had a bad experience here it usually involves people who do not live in Vallarta. I also liked the fact that Vallarta is a city with a rich history, not a created tourist town like Cancun or Ixtapa. With its red tile roofs, whitewashed buildings, and its true colonial look, Puerto Vallarta is a lovely, but authentic, Mexican town."

She finally decided to move to PV in 1990. "I've always been an organized, Type-A personality who never caused my parents or family any problems growing up," Maria confides. "I never did anything weird, have never been arrested, and so forth, but when I announced that I was going to move to Vallarta, my parents thought I was nuts. The night before I left, I went out on the town with my brothers, and it was minus twenty degrees. I almost overslept the morning I was to leave, which I almost never do. I didn't have time to dry my hair, and it froze on the way to the airport. I knew then I had made the right decision. I also remember how I used to cry when I would leave Vallarta and have to return to the weather in Chicago."

After making the move, she recalls a life very different from the Vallarta of today. "In the early 1990s, it would take three or four days for newspapers to get to Puerto Vallarta, satellite television was found mainly in the bars, and telephones weren't plentiful. In fact, when I wanted to go out, I would walk over to a friend's house to ask them if they wanted to go out because telephones were not that available. But that's how you got close to people. And, when I wanted to call my parents, I would have to go to a public calling place and wait in line to use the phone. Thankfully, communication services here have improved greatly in the last eighteen years. The Internet has really made a difference."

When Maria first moved to PV, she had no plans whatsoever to practice law. She just wanted to live here and then would figure out what she could do and what she wanted to do. She traveled throughout Mexico her first year to see if she liked other areas within the country better than PV. She had always been a city girl and thought she might move to Mexico City or Guadalajara, but that was not to be. Her first instincts were correct, and she decided to put down roots in Puerto Vallarta.

Most of the expats at the time Maria arrived in PV supported themselves by either selling time-shares or teaching English. This was before the real estate business really gained traction and began to employ a lot of Americans and Canadians. Her first job was teaching English at the hotels. She would go from hotel to hotel, timing her visits for either the start or end of work so classes were convenient for the workers. The human resources departments of the hotels would employ her to teach varying levels of English. She enjoyed teaching, but through her work with the hotels found a better opportunity as the assistant to the operations manager of the Los Tules hotel's condominium business.

"That's really when my Spanish improved significantly," Maria recalls. "I had taken two semesters of Spanish at the University of Illinois and had always been good at languages. I took seven years of French, studied German in both high school and college, and took Russian for a while because I had wanted to do a semester in Leningrad during my junior year at Illinois." Even with some Spanish, though, Maria found that the best way to learn the language was to tell people not to speak to her in English. She found that immersion is always the best way. "I would buy a newspaper and use my Spanish/English dictionary to read it. It often would take me a week to read the newspaper. I would also go to the nightclubs and just listen to people speak so my ear could get accustomed to the language. Watching television news and soap operas in Spanish also helped. I really knew I 'got it' when someone told a joke in Spanish at a nightclub and I laughed."

Maria soon discovered that everything she did in PV opened a door for her. Teaching English at the hotels opened the door to her job with Los Tules. Then, through a contact at the hotel, she got a job as an assistant to Brock Squires, the owner and operator of the La Costa Coldwell Banker real estate agency. Working as his personal assistant, she soon made a contact that helped her get work at the construction company, Grupo Playa del Sol, where she worked from 1998 to 2003. She did a lot of legal advising for the company because of its financial relationships with U.S. clients and U.S.-style loan agreements. Maria had experience with both financial relationships and loan agreements from her work at the Chicago law firm, so she was able to help the company understand how those agreements would fit with Mexican law.

Work was going great at that time, but in 1999 Maria felt a strong urge to return to the classroom to enhance her skills. She paid a visit to the Centro Estudios Universatarios Arcos, the first accredited university in Puerto Vallarta and a private school affiliated with the Polytechnic University in Mexico City. She asked the director if she could audit a history class, but he told her that they didn't really have any classes she could audit. In fact, most of the majors were specific to the needs of the local market, more bread and butter degrees like accounting, business administration, and law. He recommended that she work towards a law degree, which she did. Maria, in addition to her day job, spent five hours a day, five days a week, for three years in school and graduated in 2002 with her Mexican law degree. The cost was just six hundred pesos per month. "It was a challenge since I had to do everything in Spanish," Maria laughs. "Luckily, I have always loved school and done well. I graduated second in my class."

By 2003 Grupo Playa del Sol's outside legal firm decided to open an office in Puerto Vallarta, and Maria was hired to work in that office. It opened in the fall of 2003 and was an immediate success. She mainly did corporate work and real estate, but because she was an American and understood Mexican law well, she had many clients who were interested in investing in Puerto Vallarta as well as other locations within Mexico. She concentrated on working with condo associations, house purchases, investments, structuring of corporations for tax purposes, and business planning. Of the clients she acquired for the firm, about 90 percent were foreigners, mainly Americans.

But after four years in the law office, Maria could no longer resist and took the full-time plunge into a very hot real estate market by becoming Tropicasa Real Estate's in-house attorney in the fall of 2007. Joining the firm was an easy decision since the owner of the firm had been her good friend for many years, and Maria was ready for a new challenge.

Now, helping primarily Americans and Canadians become homeowners in Mexico became Maria's full-time job. "I think it is important for those who want to purchase down here, as well as those who already live here, to know something about the Mexican legal system for their own protection. Mexico's legal system is based on Napoleonic law, which in turn is based on Roman law. It's codified law, which means that whatever is not in the law is not allowed, and whatever is prohibited in the law is prohibited..There should be no gray areas, but that is not always the case. The litigation system, for example: a lawsuit or criminal proceeding has no jury. You probably won't even see the judge. It's all written, and there is no oral argument. It can be complicated, and there is a lot of corruption to deal with within the system. Corruption, of course, is not specific only to Mexico, but it is very real here."

That may change eventually. Mexico's President Calderón signed legislation in June of 2008 designed to fundamentally change Mexico's system of justice, allowing for U.S.-style oral trials and establishing a presumption of innocence for all criminal defendants. Under the new law, however, the changes need not be fully implemented until 2016.

Maria strongly believes that understanding local law is essential to making the best of living here. "There is a saying here: 'Better to have a bad agreement than a good fight,'" she says. "For every lawyer that tells you that it's going to cost you more to prove your point than it's worth, you've got nine lawyers who will take your money and set you down a path where you may eventually win after years of litigation and expense. I think if people know some of this information in advance, especially labor laws, they will be better prepared to deal with the system."

"For example," Maria cautions, "Americans, Canadians, and other foreigners who buy real estate in Mexico often run into labor problems. Labor law is the number one area where they can get in trouble. In Mexico, labor laws favor the employee. If it is one person's word against another's, they are going to believe the employee. Knowing what you are getting into when you hire a maid, a gardener, or other service workers helps provide you with a worst-case scenario so you won't be surprised."

Maria adds that if you ask someone verbally to come to work for you and to work *only* for you, once he or she starts work, that is as good as a written contract in Mexico. "Make sure you have their duties and all the work details in writing. Once hired, people have all the rights and privileges, like severance, proportionate vacation time, and Christmas bonus. If you don't pay, they can sue you and you must continue to pay their salary until a decision is made through a court of law. Always pay severance. It is pay for ninety days of work, any vacation time they have coming, and their Christmas bonus. If you don't pay severance, you will probably be sued. It's as simple as that."

Maria feels strongly about providing both newcomers and expats currently living in Vallarta information about the legal system and their rights. "I've seen too many situations that could have been avoided if people had a better understanding of Mexican law. A prime example of things people don't understand is how cultural perception enters into the equation. If someone steals from you in the states, it's pretty clear-cut what to do. Not so here. Say, for example, your maid steals from you. To justify terminating the maid, you must first prove before the court of law that she stole from you and then use that legal decision to justify termination and exonerate you from paying severance. During the time you are trying to prove that the maid stole from you, the maid's daily wages accrue under the law. If you cannot conclusively prove that the maid stole from you, or if the final labor hearing is scheduled before the criminal case is resolved, you will be on the hook for the full amount of accrued severance. The lesson here is to consider not prosecuting and pay severance. I think you will find it cheaper in the long run to forget it. Always count on paying severance, and focus more on establishing a better security system within your house."

Another area of litigation Maria sees a lot when dealing with Americans and Canadians is "stop constructions," meaning suing people who build construction that is in front of your house, taller than the law allows, or that blocks views. "When clients ask me what the city regulations are regarding what can be built, I tell them, 'You know what, depending upon how much money they have, they can build whatever they want.' I can tell you what the zoning laws are, but in reality, if people want to build something, they will. The only way you can guarantee your view is by buying that piece of land yourself."

Maria's final piece of advice to someone who lives in Puerto Vallarta or is thinking about buying down here is to pay your taxes. "It's primarily the people who have investment property here who rent it out and don't register with Hacienda, which is the Mexican IRS," she says. "If you generate income in Mexico, you must pay taxes on that income. The government is really cracking down on this. If the real property is located in Mexico, it generates tax here. In January of 2008, the new flat tax went into effect with the rate in 2008 set at 16.5 percent and increasing to 17 percent in 2009 and 17.5 percent in 2010. Everyone who rents out property will be subject to the flat tax as well as the traditional income tax and will pay the higher of the two. Hacienda is actively looking for and contacting all owners who rent their properties to be sure they register. However, whatever is paid in Mexico can be credited on tax owed in the U.S. or Canada, as authorized by the tax treaties between the countries. They have your name and address, so be warned."

"Don't leave your brain at the border and come down here and think things are done that differently. They're not, especially when you're buying property," Maria exclaims. "Do everything you would do back home. Do your due diligence, use escrow, hire a lawyer if you don't feel you're being well represented by your real estate agent, and don't be afraid to ask questions."

Maria has always lived near the Cuale River and in rental places. "I love it downtown; it feels like Mexico and is the real soul of Vallarta, I think. I now live on the hill above downtown, about a block north of the Cuale. It's the neighborhood that borders 'gringo gulch.' I live in a *casita* right behind the main cathedral. It is a part of the house that the American film director John Huston rented when he was here in the 1960s to film *The Night of the Iguana*. The street I live on is primarily stairs, which is very funny when people ask where they should park when they visit me. I always tell them, 'That would be quite a trick considering there are stairs and no real street. It's either eighty-five steps up or twenty-five stairs down to my place; you make the choice.' It's the oldest section of Vallarta, the first settled when the town was founded."

Like many who live in PV, she has met other expats through charity work, special events, and other local activities, of which there are many. "I have found that a great way to meet people is to take classes or join specific-focus clubs, like the club for writers, the duplicate bridge club, and others. You can find out about painting classes, Spanish language classes, dance lessons, and other activities through the clubs and charities, local English language newspapers and magazines, or some of the local online sites. There is something for everyone here, especially during high season from November through April."

In fact, there are so many things to do in high season, Maria finds it's hard to keep track of them all. "On Wednesday nights, the local art galleries participate in the Art Walk, where you can visit a number of galleries, view their offerings, and sample a little cheese and wine. Also, each November, Vallarta's top-rung restaurants hold their ten-day Gourmet Festival. Participating restaurants offer special menus created by visiting chefs from around the world. The Vallarta Film Festival follows in December with a four-day event for film buffs. Wine and jazz lovers can also look forward to their own events later in the season."

Vallarta is also a good jumping-off point for a lot of interesting places within several hours of the city, Maria notes. In the mountains east of PV, the old silver and gold mining towns of San Sebastian del Oeste and Mascota are less than a two-hour drive. "It's beautiful in the mountains and quiet. There also are many lovely beaches and neat little towns on the north shore all the way up to San Blas in the state of Nayarit, which is also about a two-hour drive," she says.

And, getting there needn't be a hassle or expensive, according to Maria. "Bus travel within Mexico is absolutely amazing. I'm not talking about the city buses, but the ETN inter-city buses. They're like riding in the first class section of an airplane. Buses are on time, they run often, they're not expensive, they give you movies, they feed you, they provide air conditioning and a nice bathroom, and the legroom they provide is exceptional. When I was working at the law firm and had to go to Guadalajara on business often, I would catch the bus at midnight, get in to Guadalajara at around five in the morning, go have breakfast, do my business, do a little shopping, and then hop on the six o'clock bus to return to PV, which got me in around 11:00 p.m. I could sleep on the bus, so it worked out very well and cost me under a hundred dollars for a round trip ticket. If I had driven, it would have been around a four-and-a-half-hour drive with over thirty dollars in tolls each way, and I would have been exhausted and probably would have had to stay overnight. Flying would have cost well over three hundred dollars and included all of the usual airport hassles, including taxis to and from each airport."

As a long-time resident of Vallarta, planning and the environment are of deep interest to Maria. She likes to be involved with her adopted city and often attends local planning meetings to keep an eye on officials to ensure that they are responsibly planning for the future. The city recently brought in a planning firm from Spain that compared that country's Andalucia province to the state of Jalisco, where PV is located. The Spanish planning team said Puerto Vallarta is going through what Andalucia went through ten years ago, especially their coastal cities like Marbella. They were brought in to help with the planning for the development south of Puerto Vallarta, between the Bay of Banderas and Barra de Navidad in the state of Jalisco. Key to the recommended plan was the building of a Highway 200 bypass route around Puerto Vallarta to alleviate city traffic congestion. The Spanish planning team also recommended a new business district close to the airport—more toward Las Juntas and Ixtapa—that would house government offices, banks, and other businesses. That would leave the downtown area primarily for retail shops and restaurants and significantly improve the parking situation, especially during high season.

Since Maria moved to PV nearly twenty years ago, she thinks the city has actually gotten cleaner. There is certainly more environmental awareness and concern for the ecology, which the new city administration is stressing. New recycling laws have been passed which require separation of trash. She also likes the emphasis the city has placed on restoring the historical district, which they've determined extends from the sports stadium on the north side of town across from the Sheraton hotel to the Conchas Chinas neighborhood on the south side of town. "I like to call it the 'Carmelization of Vallarta,'" she says. "I don't consider that a pejorative. Carmel, California, has done a great job in maintaining that special 'look and feel' that you associate with Carmel, a very classy place. We're doing the same here, and I love it."

CHAPTER THREE

DEBRA OLD

Widow
Penticton, British Columbia
Owner/Operator Hacienda Esperanza de La Galera

"Mexico is for those of us who are running away from
something and those who are running to something."

The journey to paradise started on a Saskatchewan prairie
farm for baby boomer Debra Old. Born in the small town of
Davidson in 1954, Deb grew up surrounded by miles of wheat
fields and meandering cows, working long hours on the family farm. When she reached her senior year in high school, her
family moved to the Okanagan Valley in British Columbia,
east of Vancouver. But, Davidson remained in her heart, so she
returned to the prairie, got married, and raised her three kids
on a farm. As her children grew, Deb divorced, got a degree in
business administration at the community college in Vermil-
ion, Alberta, and started work in Stettler, Alberta, as an assistant town administrator. After six months, she started a series
of sales jobs, selling business machines to companies primarily
in the oil industry in Alberta. While in college, she met her
second husband Jim, who was in oil industry sales.

Jim and Deb decided to retire early and chose Penticton, British Columbia—five hours east of Vancouver—when Jim hit his mid-fifties. They found a beautiful home in the mountains overlooking Okanagan Lake where the valley climate was relatively benign, influenced by the surrounding mountains and the very large lake.

But the tranquil life of retirement on the lake was not to be. Soon after moving to Penticton, they discovered Jim had cancer. Within a few months he was gone, and Deb—still in her mid-forties—had to decide what to do with the rest of her life.

She and Jim had been coming to Puerto Vallarta on vacation since 1982. "It was so inexpensive then," Deb remembers. "For very little money, you could have a great time, and there were far fewer tourists back then. Jim would laugh because you could take back three empty bottles and get a free beer at a local corner store by the hotel we stayed at. He often remarked, 'What a great country.'"

They went to a Mexican fiesta on that first trip and agreed that the people seemed to be happy all of the time. "Even if you didn't speak Spanish, they welcomed you," Deb says. "Jim loved coming to Vallarta. As a matter of fact, PV was Jim's choice for a vacation, right before he passed away."

During their trips south, the couple purchased a time-share. "It was great back then. You didn't have to fight off the time-share people like you do now. I think that's one of the more negative experiences now when coming to Vallarta. What the poor tourists have to go through at the airport is terrible." Owning the time-share and loving the sunshine and warm weather, Deb decided Puerto Vallarta would be a nice place to live, a little bit of tropical paradise to heal her emotional wounds.

Recently widowed and in her mid-forties, Deb moved to Vallarta in 2000. The move was not based on anything she had researched or read, but was based more on an emotional connection she had developed over the years they had been coming to PV on vacation.

"When I came down and stayed at the time-share in 2000, I saw a local ad in a newspaper for a house priced at eighty thousand dollars," Deb recalls. "It looked nice in the ad, so I began to think about what it would be like to live in PV, but I went back to Canada without ever looking at the house." The house stuck in her mind, though. She talked to her best friend Helen about the house and the possibility of moving to Puerto Vallarta when she returned home. Getting a green light from her friend, they flew back to PV to take a close look at the house, which, of course, was much better in the picture than in person. Undaunted, she talked to a real estate agent who showed her available properties and, ultimately, the house she purchased.

"It was more about listening to my heart than a lot of objective research," she says. "It was time for me to make a move. I didn't want to live where I was living any more. My new home was bathed in sunshine, had a school next door where I could hear the kids laughing, and it was a nice place to help me heal."

She liked the local neighborhood, called a *colonia* in Spanish. Las Gaviotas means "the sea gulls" in the local language, and she liked the neighborhood because she was from the prairies of Canada and wanted a flat area in which to live. Las Gaviotas is an upscale neighborhood just east of the city's northern hotel zone and very close to many amenities and entertainment. The city is divided into a number of *colonias,* each with a distinctive character. "Most of my neighbors are professional people with families. Las Gaviotas was also close to the Sheraton hotel, where my husband and I stayed during our vacations in PV, so I knew the area." She also knew the neighborhood was safe and quiet. "An added benefit to living in Las Gaviotas is the close proximity of the local police sub-station. They drive down the streets prior to any major storm that has potential to cause damage and let you know that it is coming."

Even though Deb loves her house, she admits there are a few negatives to living where she does. "The cobblestone streets of Las Gaviotas, charming as they are, produce a lot of dust, which finds its way in copious amounts onto the furniture in houses and parked cars." This is a long-standing problem in all sections of Vallarta with similar street construction. The absence of large swaths of parks and green belt areas and the lack of city street cleaning exacerbate the dust problem.

"When I was buying my house, I spoke with the real estate agent—who was fluent in English—to see if I could get some help in examining the structure," Deb says. "Several local people came out to look at the roof and the other areas of construction to make sure the house was sound before I put my money down. Once I bought the house, though, the best source for local information turned out to be a woman who had lived in my neighborhood for years. Vicky moved here when she was in her forties and is now in her eighties. If you have any questions or problems, you just call Vicky, and she will say, 'Just go talk to so and so for your answer.'"

After settling in to her new house in Las Gaviotas, Deb found that the most important lesson to learn for living in Puerto Vallarta was to establish a network of friends, particularly those who have lived in Vallarta for a while, because they provide the answers to most of your questions, from who to fix your plumbing problems to where to get the best price for produce. She discovered that the local network was indispensable for daily living.

"In addition to my local network of friends, I also rely on online information," Deb says. "The amount of information available now is very different from when I moved here eight years ago. There now are many local online sources, like the message boards at http://todopuertovallarta.yuku.com. They have multiple boards from the "All Vallarta" main board to the "Best of PV" board to keep you up-to-date. It's a great source of local news and tips on how to get the best from living in Vallarta. You have to be careful, though. Sometimes rumors masquerade as facts."

When Deb moved to Vallarta eight years ago, it was a very different place. She remembers how quiet it was with far fewer cars, a simpler life, and not nearly as many expats. "When I first moved here, I had high expectations, and fortunately PV met every one of them. Coming here was so emotional for me. I found that I just loved the city. The first minute I saw it during our first vacation here those many years ago, I fell in love with it. Actually, the first time we came down, I got sick from eating shrimp and had to have a doctor come to our hotel to give me a shot. I told my husband then, 'If I die, just leave me here; don't take me back to Canada because I'm finally warm.'"

One of the things she loved about moving to Puerto Vallarta was its safety. She could walk downtown alone and not have to worry. She could walk along the downtown Malecon boardwalk and enjoy the ocean without fear. She also loved the idea that her kids could get on a plane in Canada and be at her house in five hours. She liked her garden and the fact that she could plant a papaya tree and pick her own fruit when it was ripe. She liked the music and the Mexican love of music. If there was a fiesta in her neighborhood, she could enjoy the Mariachi music from several blocks away, knowing that all Mexican celebrations call for music to be played at the highest decibel level. They didn't like it any other way.

Deb did notice a few things about the culture, though, that she found hard to get used to. The Latin male macho dominance attitude that remains in Mexico required a whole different approach for her. The house she bought was a fixer-upper and required local tradesmen to do the work. She discovered that the men she hired to work on her house were not very responsive at first. Deb would instruct them to do specific work, but often she found they would not do as told. She soon learned that within the Mexican culture, a woman does not tell a man what to do. Deb had to learn to tell the workers what to do by first asking for their help in solving a problem. She would ask, "What would happen if I had a leak in the sliding door?" They would respond with the solution, and she would reply: "Oh, could you? That would be wonderful!" "That's how things get done," Deb says. "That's how it was eight years ago, and it hasn't changed much since then."

Deb cites another example of the macho male culture at work. "Something extraordinary happens when the normally mild-mannered Mexican male gets behind the wheel of his car. In self-defense, I found that I have to become equally macho when I get behind the wheel of my car. You have to be very aggressive behind the wheel, but at the same time learn to drive defensively. I know it's paradoxical, but that's the way it is here. It isn't that there are fewer traffic laws; we have as many traffic laws here as anywhere else, but it's just that most local drivers don't pay attention to them. Puerto Vallarta—according to my Mexican friends—is the worst city in Mexico to drive in, even worse than Mexico City." Deb further cautions that you should not expect local drivers to stop when a pedestrian is in a cross-walk. "Always assume that cars have priority. Buses, by the way, are an even worse problem than cars. They race each other to see who can get to the next bus stop first, primarily because there are too many buses on the same routes all competing for the same customer."

As testimony to PV's chaotic car culture, the city—many claim—also has the distinction of having more speed bumps—called *topes* in Spanish—per traffic mile than any other city in Mexico. In fact, the PV director of transit has proclaimed that the local streets are saturated with speed bumps; most are not well installed or painted properly, and many are not even approved by city authorities. Because of the *topes*, most people drive SUVs or trucks that are high enough to clear the speed bumps without scraping or damaging the bottom of the vehicle.

Aside from a few negatives associated with the continuing macho aspect of Mexican culture, Deb thinks the local culture has many wonderful sides to it. "If you are living alone—especially if the Mexican people know you are a widow—they look after you to make sure you are okay. For example, my home was broken into once, and a man came about 11:00 p.m. on a Sunday night to make sure my doors could lock. He didn't have to do that, but he did because he was concerned for my safety."

The Mexican culture also breeds a strong sense of family and caring. "One of the things I really like is the 'hug' factor in Mexico," Deb smiles. "In Canada, we don't hug that much. In PV, I get at least a hug a day, and I really like it. The people are warm and demonstrative and care about their families and each other. Family takes precedent to almost everything, and it's so joyous to watch the extended families enjoy each other."

Living the culture to the fullest means learning the language. "I firmly believe that one of the best ways to get the most out of living in Vallarta or anywhere else in Mexico is learning Spanish. I decided early on that I wanted to be able to walk to my local corner store and be able to exchange pleasantries with them, rather than brusquely ask for what I wanted and leave." Deb took a two-week Spanish language instruction class when she first moved to PV to learn the basics and then dedicated herself to practicing with the people who work for her and others she interacts with on a daily basis. "That's how you really learn to speak the language. It's pretty much a necessity to be able to communicate with domestic service workers, since most don't speak English. However, because Puerto Vallarta is an international resort city with over four million visitors each year, about half American and Canadian, English is widely spoken."

Having lived in Vallarta for eight years, Deb knows that not everything about PV is completely rosy. "There are things about living in PV that I don't really like, such as the paperwork required to get anything done. It's is getting better, but something like renewing a visa is still difficult and requires the dedication of the better part of a day to complete. In fact, a local service industry has sprung up to help expats avoid the interminable lines and crush of people at the Mexican immigration office. For about a hundred and fifty dollars at visa renewal time each year, these companies will handle the whole process." Standing in line at the bank when they have just one cashier but twenty people standing in line is another of Deb's pet peeves that helps to take a little of the shine off Vallarta.

Aside from those minor inconveniences that Deb admits can be the bane of consumers anywhere, she still thinks that life is pretty darned good in paradise. Vallarta's blessed sunshine and perennial summertime seem to ensure that Deb is rarely ill, but she does have peace of mind knowing that the local health care community is top notch. Since her health care coverage in Canada does not extend to Mexico, she had to purchase a health care plan locally. "I bought an international policy based on the recommendation of my local banker and pay about twelve hundred dollars a year for coverage," she says. "I don't really know how good the policy is since, fortunately, I have been very healthy and haven't had to use it. Plus, medical costs are so reasonable here that I pay all my medical and dental costs out-of-pocket." She did use a local hospital when she had a very bad case of influenza. Deb thought it was excellent, and the costs were "beyond reasonable." Most physicians charge around fifty dollars for an office visit.

"I have my annual physicals done at Cornerstone Hospital, which is just five minutes from my house," Deb explains. "Cornerstone is very well equipped with all of the latest medical technology. My personal physician is excellent and speaks perfect English, as many health care professionals do in Vallarta. They do all of the same tests I had done in Canada."

She has found that good dentists are plentiful, also. Deb uses one just around the corner from her house. A one-hour cleaning and checkup is just thirty-five dollars. Deb has friends from Canada who come to Puerto Vallarta to get their teeth fixed because the work is excellent, and it costs about one-third of what it would cost them back home.

Most of Deb's day-to-day relationships involve expat community friends she has met. When she first moved to Vallarta, she didn't know how to meet people. So, Deb decided to go to the bars, traditionally where lots of people go looking for companionship. But, Deb found that she didn't really like the people she met at the bars. "So many would go just for happy hour, and I didn't want to do that. I came back home and played the piano for a while to get my courage up to try again. I decided to go to an AA (Alcoholics Anonymous) meeting because those people don't get drunk or at least are trying not to get drunk. I didn't like the bar crowd and thought that sober people were probably more interesting people. That's where I met my four best friends, and we're still best friends."

When she first moved to PV, Deb also discovered the International Friendship Club (IFC), but found most of the members were couples and, as a single, felt a little uncomfortable.

Being single forced her to get out of the house and find ways to connect with people, and charity groups, special events, and monthly newcomer breakfasts provided the best avenues to meet people and establish new relationships.

One of the other ways she decided to get out of the house and stay busy was to become an entrepreneur, like so many other baby boomers who retire or just move to Vallarta for the adventure. "After I bought my house, it took two or three years to get it fixed up to the point where I was happy with it. Then I had lots of friends and relatives come down to visit me. But, two years ago, I started to get a little bored and began looking at other properties. I looked up the north coast to Sayulita and then other areas farther north, but nothing struck my eye."

Every winter, though, Deb would take two or three people up to the cool Sierra Madre mountain town of San Sebastian del Oeste, east of Puerto Vallarta at an elevation of about forty-three hundred feet. The road was not very good then, and it took longer than the hour and a half it takes now. They would have a beer and look around and then go the main plaza to buy the delicious organic coffee that was grown on the small plantations around San Sebastian. On one of her trips, she noticed a sign on the front of a building in the main plaza. It was a For Sale by Owner sign with a picture of an old hacienda. The ad piqued Deb's interest, so she called the owner who invited them over for a tour of the old hacienda.

"As we approached the property, my companions told me, 'You have to be out of your mind,'" Deb laughs. "Of course, at that time the road was not paved, there were lots of curves and rocks, and it was a little challenging getting from the town plaza to the hacienda. Once the hacienda came into view, though, my friends recanted and told me, 'If you have enough money, just buy it.' I fell in love with the place and the setting, but my friend Helen sealed the deal for me. I trust her judgment, and if she felt comfortable, then I knew it was the right thing to do. I wanted a place my family and friends could come, where they could relax and really enjoy the time spent."

The hacienda certainly was a cure for Deb's boredom. It was a major fixer-upper, and she has been very busy since she bought it bringing it up to the quality level of a first-class bed and breakfast. It sits on four acres in the valley below San Sebastian along a beautiful stream that meanders through the property. Hacienda Esperanza de La Galera opened its doors on January 1, 2008.

"My guests are people who want to see the real Mexico or have read about haciendas and have always wanted to stay at one," Deb says. "I've had Americans, Canadians, Welsh, Germans, and more affluent Mexicans stay at the hacienda. I charge a hundred dollars per night, year-round, for each of the hacienda's three suites, which includes breakfast in the morning." San Sebastian has developed into a new hot spot for day-trippers from PV. At least three tour buses a day arrive in the main plaza, plus a tour company offers day trips via a small plane.

Deb discovered that the place was a working gold and silver mining hacienda and was one of the original haciendas in San Sebastian. When the revolution began in the early 1800s, the Spanish left their gold and silver mines behind. Now, with the price of gold so high, some of the original mines are being reopened.

Managing the hacienda occupies five days a week of Deb's time now, so she is no longer bored. Because of its success, she decided to put her home in Las Gaviotas on the market and build a new house on the property in San Sebastian. "I won't leave Vallarta completely, though. I love it too much. I'll be looking for a small condo so I can split my time between San Sebastian and PV."

Back home in Vallarta for a few days during the week to pay the bills and run errands, Deb ponders the cost of living here. "When I first moved to PV in 2000, my electricity bill was about $110, billed every two months. My bill now runs around $458 for that same period of time. To counterbalance that, though, my water bill is very little, I think about $36 every two months for my home, which is over 3,000 square feet with a large pool. Property taxes on my house are less than $500 a year, which is one of the great bargains of living here."

Managing her budget also includes setting aside a few bucks a month for leisure time entertainment. "Puerto Vallarta is well known within Mexico as being second only to Mexico City for the number of top quality restaurants. The city has a wide variety to choose from. That's all good news. The bad news for those of us who live here is the cost of an evening out at one of the better restaurants now rivals most comparable U.S. and Canadian restaurants. At the top-tier restaurants, dinner for two with a bottle of wine and tip exceeds a hundred dollars. Of course, we don't always go out to top-tier restaurants because that's where tourists dine, and that's why the prices are high. Every expat has their favorite local restaurants where the food is good, the margaritas tasty, and the prices comforting."

Even when she doesn't go out to dinner, Deb likes a glass of wine now and then, but is not keen on the price of wine in PV. Wine is taxed so heavily that a bottle of wine that can be bought north of the border at a retail store for eight dollars usually sells for double and some times triple that amount in PV. One recent improvement, however, is the variety of wines that can now be purchased locally. When she first moved to Vallarta, stores like Wal-Mart, Sam's, and Costco did not exist. Those stores plus the new Liverpool department store— Mexico's largest upscale department store chain—have brought a larger diversity of wine, including brands from Europe, South

America, and a much better representation of U.S. wineries, instead of primarily domestic Mexican wine.

Besides wine, Deb notes, new cars are more expensive by about 20 percent, good quality furniture is about the same as north of the border, and she says expect to pay double for consumer electronics. "A friend of mine just purchased a large screen, fifty-inch plasma television and paid twenty-eight hundred dollars for it," Deb reveals. "He told me that same set at major consumer electronics stores in the U.S. was retailing for sixteen-hundred dollars at the time he bought it. Ah, the price of paradise."

Housing, though, is one budget item that truly still remains a great value in PV, Deb believes. Her home currently is listed for $525,000 and is 3,300 square feet on a nearly quarter acre lot. The house has a large patio and pool in a very quiet, upscale neighborhood close to the beach and everything else. The only caveat is lot size. Land is very expensive in this international resort city, so lots tend to be quite small in comparison with average lot sizes in the U.S. and Canada.

When she moved to PV, she bought a 2002 Nissan car, which costs her less than thirty dollars a year for its annual registration. But she found out that buying and registering the car in Mexico and having local plates on her car had benefits way beyond the cost of ownership. "I don't get singled-out for attention by the local traffic police nearly as much as those cars with U.S. or Canadian plates, which can be a problem for many who live here," Deb warns. "If you do get stopped by the transit police for speeding, do not attempt to bribe the traffic officer. *La mordida*—"the bite" in Spanish—is well known throughout Mexico as a means for police officers to enhance their low salaries. However, it's less expensive to give the officer your driver's license (they will take one of your license plates if you don't have your license with you) as requested and then go to the local station in Las Juntas by the international airport to pay the fine and retrieve your license. If you pay the fine within fifteen days of issuance, you'll get a 50 percent discount off the cost of the fine."

"I have had not problems with the police. In fact, they have been very helpful to me," she says. "My house was broken into and all of my jewelry stolen around ten in the morning on a Sunday during *Semana Santa*, the Easter holy week in Catholic Mexico. Crime increases dramatically during this time because the city is flooded with vacationers from both inside and outside of Mexico. Professional gangs from outside of the area come to PV to prey upon the crowds. I called the police, and they came right away and were very helpful, although they were not able to recover my jewelry. The gang that robbed my house was from Talpa, a small town in the Sierra Madre east of Puerto Vallarta. I know because I came home and surprised them as they were leaving. They were very well dressed and hopped my fence, but left a cell phone with all Talpa telephone numbers. Unfortunately they were long gone by the time the police arrived."

"Another well-known favorite technique used by pickpockets during *Semana Santa* is to approach someone from behind on a busy street, throw mustard on their back, and then run up to help the person clean the mustard off," Deb continues. "It's usually a two-person operation, with one cleaning and the other cleaning out the victim's pockets. Most of us locals try to avoid going out that much during *Semana Santa* or just leave town."

Deb spends five days a week at the hacienda and is happy to avoid the increasing traffic of the city. The growth of Vallarta has changed the way Deb lives, to a degree. She doesn't drive to the downtown area nearly as much as she used to, relying more frequently now on buses and taxis so she can also avoid the downtown parking problems and have a libation or two at dinner without worry. The city has built three new downtown parking structures, but the increasing crush of vehicles in the central area of Puerto Vallarta continues to outpace parking.

"With the significant increase in the number of cars, trucks, and buses, air pollution has gotten much worse since I first moved to the area," she laments. "Compounding the problem, Vallarta is situated between the Bay of Banderas and the Sierra Madre mountains, which traps the pollution, similar to the Los Angeles basin in California. I can really tell the difference when I leave San Sebastian's cool, clean mountain air and return to PV."

After eight years in PV, Deb, like many other boomers who fled the cold north for the warmth of paradise, has made the adjustments necessary to mainstream her life into Mexico. "I feel so at home here," she says contentedly. "I just received my Mexican citizenship and am as happy as I could possibly be."

For those contemplating making a similar move to Puerto Vallarta, Deb offers this advice: "Just remember, you're not in Kansas any more. You're coming to some place different, and it is someone else's country. They've lived this way for years and years, and they didn't invite us. Don't try to make it into 'the way it was back home' and expect things to function in the manner you are accustomed to. This is not our country, and if we are lucky, we get invited in to stay."

"A Mexican once told me that there are two kinds of people who come to Mexico: Those of us who are running away from something, the ones who spend all of their time at happy hour, and those who are running to something. I ran to something: the place I fell in love with so many years ago."

CHAPTER FOUR

KRYSTAL FROST

Married
Missoula, Montana
Owner/Operator Body and Sol

"I was looking for a place to land where I could use my
skills and develop a lifestyle, and Vallarta just reached
out and embraced me."

Krystal Frost was a baby boomer flower child raised in the
California desert. Born in Bakersfield in 1954, her dad was an
ophthalmologist who moved Krystal, her bank officer mother,
and two brothers to Palm Desert, where she graduated from
high school at the tender age of 15. After receiving her diploma,
she headed to San Francisco—the epicenter of her movement—
to join like-minded flower children during that famous summer of Woodstock. Soon tiring of that scene, she migrated farther up the coast to cool, rainy British Columbia for the rest of
the summer.

When that summer of peace and love came to an end, Krystal moved east and enrolled at the University of Toronto. She
studied anthropology and history for two years and gave birth to
her first son before returning to British Columbia to finish her
anthropology degree at Simon Fraser University in Vancouver.

Following graduation, she applied for graduate school at Pontificia Universidad Javeriana in Bogota, Colombia, and was accepted, even though she spoke no Spanish at the time and the curriculum was entirely in Spanish. She left her son with her parents in California and then flew to Bogota to begin her graduate program.

Six months after Krystal started graduate school, she saw what she thought was an easy way to make ten thousand dollars, so she took an offer to become a drug carrier—a "mule"—to transport cocaine to the United States. She was caught at the airport and spent the next two years in a Columbian prison for women. "I never was into drugs myself, other than the normal experimentation all kids did at the time," Krystal admits. "They say that any dealings with cocaine is bad karma. There were a few other English-speaking women in the prison, so we all banded together. It was like something straight out of the movie *Midnight Express*. I was only the second person convicted of that crime in Colombia. At that time, they usually just slapped your hands and deported you, but this was during Nixon's 'War on Crime,' so they made an example of me." After her release from prison, Krystal worked at the U.S. Embassy in Bogota for a year, specializing in helping distressed Americans, which included contact with Americans held in Columbian prisons.

Loving Latin America's rich and diverse cultures, Krystal decided to travel the continent to see what living was like in the different South American countries. Now fluent in Spanish, she started in Argentina and held a variety of jobs there and in Peru and Ecuador. "I spent eight years in South America during an interesting but politically insecure time. I studied in several of the countries and had a wide variety of jobs that included working as a waitress, modeling, theater, and work as an interpreter at American embassies." During her sojourn in

Latin America, Krystal's son and father often would join her during vacations.

Krystal has always been drawn to Latin cultures. "When I was a child, I used to have a vision of myself as this little brown person, wearing a long skirt and huaraches, named Maria. When I played with other little girls, I would become Maria. Maybe I was Maria in a past life."

In 1981 Krystal and her alter ego Maria returned to California to live with her parents and son. She worked in her dad's office for a year but then started getting restless again. Her former college roommate was now the president of Hearst Films in Los Angeles and was working on a movie being shot in Montana called *Walks Far Woman*, which starred Raquel Welch. She offered Krystal a job as an assistant director, and soon she was in Billings, Montana. The film was shot on the Crow Indian Reservation south of Billings. Krystal's job as an anthropologist was to work with the local indigenous people. She got to know and admire one of the Crow families—the Buffalo Bulltails—during the shoot. The women invited her to their home and then to their sweat lodge—a form of ritual sauna. While she and the other women were purifying their bodies, the mother of the family asked if she would like to meet one of her boys. John Frost and Krystal were immediately attracted to each other, soon married, and had two daughters.

John and Krystal remained in the Billings area for a few years while Krystal taught anthropology at the Billings extension of Montana State University. She learned the history and the culture of America's indigenous people through the eyes of her husband and his people. In 1984, they moved to Missoula in western Montana to follow John's job as an electrical line inspector. It also was an opportunity to distance John from the influence of alcoholism on the reservation. When the girls were two and four, Krystal returned to work at the University of

Montana, working with the Sports Foundation to bring young and promising athletes from all over the country to the school to participate in sports.

While in Missoula, Krystal became interested in the hospitality business, left the University of Montana, and became the director of sales for the Red Lion Corporation. She and John bought ten acres of land outside of town on the Clarks River and built a home for their family.

Life on the ranch, though, did not last for Krystal and her kids. John's alcoholism had taken a toll on the family, so she decided to take the girls to the land she loved: Latin America. She longed for the languid life south of the border, but even more importantly, she wanted to give her kids the advantage of being reared in a culturally rich environment where they could learn a second language. South America, though, was too far away from friends and family, so she got out her map, looked at Hawaii's latitude, and drew a straight line to Puerto Vallarta on Mexico's west central coast. She had been to Hawaii on vacation and loved the climate. Puerto Vallarta offered both the climate and the culture she adored, so they began packing their bags.

Krystal had done no research on Puerto Vallarta before she jumped on a plane in 1986 and flew down to live. A friend offered her a nice rental condo on the beach south of PV while she searched for a job and prepared to bring her children to Vallarta. She quickly found employment as the property manager for a large villa on a south coast beach near Garza Blanca that was owned by Americans. The large, beautiful home was host to one of Mexico's presidents during the two years Krystal managed the property. While working there, she found a live-in nanny—Maria from Chiapas—to take care of the kids, which eased her mind. "There are no better people than Latin women to take care of your kids," Krystal admires. "It was like having a wife. She taught me to make tamales in banana leaves, chiles rellenos, sauces, and the attention and rituals that Mexican women employ in their cooking. My children learned Spanish and Chiapaneca tales first hand."

Always restless, in 1988 the once flower child decided to move on and take a crack at selling time-shares, a job of both choice and necessity for most adventurous baby boomers who come to Vallarta without a job. "It worked for me. I maintained my ethics, did a good job, was mostly in the top 5 percent of performers, and had lots of satisfied customers. I didn't make as much money as the more hard-sell sales people, but I have never been driven by money." She sold time-shares for the Krystal, Velas Vallarta, and several smaller properties. The key to working for them in Krystal's mind was their more easygoing approach to time-share, no high-pressure tactics.

The hours of a time-share sales person worked perfectly for Krystal since her kids were old enough now for school. "I enrolled them in the American School in the Marina when it was just 'three rooms and mud,'" she laughs. "I kept them there for a few years and then moved them to the British American School in Las Aralias because I liked their curriculum better. The school also had a teacher that I really admired, so I made sure my kids were in her class." At that time, the British American School offered only grades K–8. Her children were in the first graduating class. She moved them back to the American School for the first two years of high school before sending them to live with her mother to finish high school in Eugene, Oregon. The girls wanted at least a few years of the "American high school experience" before they went to college. "My girls' exposure to a multi-cultural, bilingual environment and lots of hard work helped them get scholarships to good schools," Krystal says proudly.

One morning in 1994 she woke up and found she was sick and tired of selling time-shares. "Time-share is not a career. It's just something that brings you money and gets you through life. It's short term." She started her own body-healing business, utilizing the skills she had developed many years ago while attending school in Vancouver. "It was my hobby at that time. I learned shiatsu, massage, yoga, and other forms of body healing because it was kind of a flower child thing to do. I learned all about herbal and organic remedies, also, and became very good at it."

Krystal started as a yoga teacher at a hotel in the northern hotel zone doing classes on the beach and then expanded her capabilities to include massage therapy. "There were maybe two other people in all of Vallarta who were doing massage therapy back in the mid-1990s. I opened my business, Body and Sol, in 1995 in a location very near the popular Rizzo's grocery store on the south side of town. It was great for walk-in traffic and also had access to parking, which was a real plus."

Since she was a pioneer in her field and found it difficult to find products to use and sell, she searched out raw materials and developed and produced her own emollients and other products that she used and sold at Body and Sol. She also offered massage training programs for local people interested in learning the craft. "Many of the people who own massage therapy businesses in town were trained by me," she notes.

To add to her business offerings, Krystal enrolled in a first-ever acupuncture degree program at the University of Guadalajara's Puerto Vallarta campus in 2002. The three-year program was developed within the university's medical school in Guadalajara in keeping with Mexico's recognition of acupuncture and eastern medicine as accepted and certified medical practices. Krystal followed her degree in acupuncture with post-graduate study at Bastyr University, a leader in natural health science education located north of Seattle, Washington. She specialized in aesthetic acupuncture.

While studying acupuncture and natural health science, the energetic Krystal still found time to start a parallel business in 2005 called Organic Select (http://www.organic-select.com), an online store that sells organic food to consumers interested in a healthy lifestyle. Based in Vallarta, the firm works directly with local farmers to provide products for the online store. The company charges an annual membership, which brings additional benefits to members and helps support research and expand local growers. "We have customers around the bay and up the north coast. They appreciate the service because the Web site is user-friendly, and we sell hard-to-find organic products that are delivered directly to their homes. Lots of people like it because of the traffic congestion, and many don't have cars."

Krystal honed her marketing skills back in the mid-1990s when she discovered and developed the coffee business in San Sebastian del Oeste, the tiny mountain town east of Vallarta. "I work primarily from passion and inspiration, and the coffee business in San Sebastian was a true passion for me," Krystal says. Her first trip to the mountain town was in 1994. "At that time, it was a five-hour drive to San Sebastian from PV or a short flight in a rickety old plane that was held together with baling wire. There was just one place to stay in town and no restaurants." During Krystal's first trip, she wandered around San Sebastian for a while before coming upon the La Quinta hacienda. "It was such a beautiful place that I just knocked on their door because I wanted to meet them," she remembers. She didn't realize at the time that her knock on the door would open an opportunity to a passion that she pursues to this day.

After establishing a relationship with the family at the hacienda, she learned that they grew shade-grown coffee in the perfect high altitude of San Sebastian. "They had no idea what potential their business had. They had been growing these beautiful coffee beans since the 1940s on ten acres of land. I became impassioned by the care they took in the whole authentic process. They harvested all by hand, dried the beans in the sun, and took great care with each step of the process. In fact, they still do."

Krystal was so impassioned about the La Quinta coffee that she took a class on coffee growing and processing at the National Institute of Coffee in the state of Vera Cruz, the coffee center of Mexico. She took a sample of the La Quinta coffee to the institute, where they tested it and gave the coffee their highest rating, a marketer's dream. During the course, she learned the entire coffee process, including how to roast, blend, and grade the coffee beans.

Armed with her new coffee knowledge, Krystal returned to San Sebastian to help La Quinta become a well-known local coffee brand. "The first thing I recommended was the purchase of a roaster. They were using this big barrel over a fire to roast the beans that was turned by hand. So, we found a state-funded program for small coffee growers, applied for a low-interest loan, and bought a roaster in the states to help modernize and control the process. We also worked on packaging and other things to help market the product." Krystal became so involved with the coffee project that she moved into a house and lived part-time in San Sebastian while continuing to operate her business in Puerto Vallarta.

Krystal enjoys staying very busy these days with Body and Sol and her online organic food business, but she often fondly remembers the days when life here was far simpler. "So many things in Vallarta have changed during the last twenty years. It was more of a small town when I first moved here. Then, the road from the airport to downtown was just a two-lane asphalt highway, and you could find a place to park wherever and whenever you wanted to. There were a lot fewer restaurants, also, and it was easier to get in without a reservation. I really loved those days because PV had a real laid-back, small town atmosphere. Also, Punta de Mita at that time was a place we would take our kids to on a weekend to play in the caves. There weren't many people out there then, just local villages."

After years of traveling, Krystal finally found her personal paradise in PV. "I was looking for a place to land where I could use my skills and develop a lifestyle, and Vallarta just reached out and embraced me. I lived in South America, Montana, Canada, and California, but never really felt like I fit in. When I came to Vallarta, I loved the Latin culture and immediately felt at home and at ease. I also loved the international feel to the city. People from all over the world choose Vallarta. I'm glad I did."

CHAPTER FIVE

CHARLIE RONDOT

Single
Calgary, Alberta
Agent, Coldwell Banker La Costa Real Estate

"God really did a good job with this place."

Boomer Charlie Rondot entered life fifty-three years ago
in a little Ontario village of just five hundred people about
thirty miles outside of Windsor, Ontario, which is just across
the river from Detroit. It was a town where many people spoke
French, and Charlie's family was no exception, speaking both
French and English. His dad passed away when he was very
young leaving his piano teacher mom with the responsibility
to raise her seven kids by herself. When Charlie was eleven, his
family moved to Windsor where he attended high school and
then spent a few years at the University of Windsor. He took
three years of Spanish in high school, not knowing that some-
day it might come in very handy. Always athletic, Charlie was
active in sports and played city league Canadian football until
a series of injuries finally caught up with him at twenty-two.
While in school, Charlie started his long career in the restaurant business, which he continued in Toronto before hearing
the call of the wild and heading west to Calgary in 1986.

After several years of putting up with the cold, bitter Calgary winters, Charlie took his first two-week vacation to Puerto Vallarta. He didn't know much about PV other than what he had read in the travel brochures he had picked up at a local agency. When his plane touched down in PV, it was love at first sight, so much so that he returned to paradise three out of the next four years. "The beautiful winter weather in Vallarta was such a stark contrast to Calgary," Charlie remembers. I said to myself, *This is winter? People really live like this during winter?*" The sun-drenched climate was Vallarta's real appeal for Charlie, but he also loved the topography with the mountains framing the bay. He thought it was truly a beautiful place with spectacular weather to boot.

In early 1993, Charlie decided that Puerto Vallarta was the place for him. It was becoming harder each time for him to get on the plane and return home to Calgary. His decision to make the move south was mostly based on pure emotion, but he did take the time to look into whatever pre-Internet information was available at that time. "Frankly, though, I was sold on PV through experiencing it on vacation. It was a charming, small colonial city at the time I vacationed here with very warm, friendly people. It wasn't a tourist trap like Cancun or Cabo. It was a lot quieter back then with much less traffic, very unlike what we are experiencing today, with all of the rapid growth."

Charlie was lucky that he had a former coworker friend from Calgary living in Vallarta at that time who helped him find a place to live, a small *pensione* south of the Cuale River that he used as a base to look for a longer-term living situation. "I loved it," Charlie recalls, "because it was well located, quiet, and a real slice of Mexico, which was exactly what I was looking for." Within three weeks, he found a place nearby and lived there for his first three years in Puerto Vallarta.

Besides a place to live, Charlie's other key priority was finding a job to pay the bills. And, like many other adventurous pre-retirement American and Canadian baby boomers who visit and then fall in love with PV, he took a job in the time-share industry. His first four years were spent working in the sales offices of major resorts, but the high-pressure salesmanship required for time-share wore him out. "I was ready for a change, and fortunately an opportunity to work as a food and beverage manager at a hotel I was working with came up. The job fit with my past experience perfectly, so I jumped at the chance to get out of time-share sales." By this time, he had moved to an apartment near the Marina, which was much closer to his new job.

While working at the restaurant, Charlie suffered a herniated disc, the same injury he had suffered in Calgary. "I've always been athletic, and this really slowed me down. The hotel doctor looked at me and then recommended a local doctor, who recommended an MRI to see what the damage was. I required surgery to fix the problem and had the operation done at San Javier hospital by the Marina, which was really excellent. San Javier is a very modern hospital with cutting-edge technology. The total cost of the procedure was about 15% of what it would have cost in Calgary. Thankfully, I had a good international insurance plan through the hotel."

Charlie managed the hotel restaurant for nearly six years before he decided to get back into sales, this time with Coldwell Banker's local real estate office. He had been working seventy hours a week at his hotel job and wanted something different. "Lying on my back in the hospital gave me some time to think about what I wanted to do with my life, and the real estate industry seemed a good choice, especially with my time-share sales experience," Charlie reflects. "Real estate in Vallarta was really beginning to boom in 2003, and I wanted to be part of it."

Charlie explains that real estate sales in Mexico are not regulated, so salespeople working in the real estate industry are not required to be certified. Therefore, the barriers to entry for this profession are quite low. Fortunately, his four years in the time-share industry was excellent experience, so Charlie hit the ground running and is now the second-best producer for the Coldwell Banker La Costa office in Puerto Vallarta.

Even though there are no specific certification requirements for real estate people, Charlie's company requires that each sales person pass a two-hour test to certify their knowledge. "I think most good real estate companies in Vallarta train their employees, but Coldwell Banker is quite rigorous. The local real estate business is very strong, so many American and Canadian boomers work in the industry, some with previous experience and some without. One advantage I had was my Spanish language skills. I grew up bilingual, studied Spanish in school for three years, and have the good fortune to have a Mexican girlfriend. Even with all of that, I found that you don't really understand a language until you can think in it and, especially, understand the jokes. My language fluency allows me to work very well with both Mexican nationals as well as American and Canadian buyers."

When Charlie started in the real estate business, they told him to make sure he had cash on hand for six months because it takes that long to develop a revenue stream from selling real estate. He took it to heart and as a good businessman still manages his cash very conservatively. He also has always been an adventurer and entrepreneur and tends to gravitate toward businesses where his success is solely dependent upon himself. "In my real estate job, I usually work fifty to sixty hours a week, which is less than the seventy hours a week I was putting in at the hotel. That number of hours is a whole lot more manageable and allows me a little time to enjoy paradise, which is why I moved here in the first place! Real estate work is also seasonal, which helps. The heavy work period is during high season from November through April when the bulk of the Americans and Canadians are visiting. I like it because the seasonality allows me to travel during the summer, so I go to Canada every year to see my mother and relatives."

Charlie's real estate experience has been rewarding, for both remuneration as well as satisfaction. "I enjoy working with people and the pleasure it brings me in helping other boomers like myself find a place here, a place that I really love," Charlie says. "I tell my clients that one of the most important considerations when buying property in Mexico is title clearance. Here in Mexico, we have what is called *ejido* land, which is not legal. Anyone considering property in Mexico should be very careful to ensure that they don't consider *ejido* land. An *ejido* is a collective group of people who live and work on a determined piece of property as a community. It is land that was designated in 1937 for agricultural purposes and use by local farmers. Most importantly, *ejido* land is not titled. To own property with title, the land has to be 'regularized,' a process in which all of the farmers who own the particular property agree to sell it to a non-Mexican. Once this legal step has been taken, the land has become regularized, and owners can take legal title to the property. We sell only regularized property."

Charlie also points out that Americans, Canadians, and other foreigners are not permitted to own land within the restricted zone, a designated area within one hundred kilometers of any Mexican border or within eighty kilometers of any Mexican coastline. For those who purchase property within the restricted zone, property title is held within a fifty-year bank trust, for which an annual trust fee is paid. Property further inland can be owned outright.

Charlie is very aware that the baby boomer wave has hit Puerto Vallarta and sees nothing but upside for the local real estate market. "Boomers are a huge market for us now that they are looking south for the warm weather and casual lifestyles that Vallarta offers. Boomers have the cash from their home equity, which is a good thing because this is still pretty much a cash market. About 10 percent of the homes sold down here are financed, usually at interest rates about 2 percent higher than comparable rates north of the border. Financing became available about four years ago with regulatory changes that allowed the home in Mexico to be used as collateral. But, most boomer purchasers are buying second homes for retirement with home equity loans on their current properties in the U.S. and Canada. Some even have multiple homes in other international resort areas and are just adding another destination to their portfolios."

Charlie thinks that sales especially to Americans are slowing somewhat because of the housing market problems in the U.S., but he says the Canadian dollar and overall economy in that country is doing well, so that market continues to be strong. Another key positive factor for the local real estate market he cites is the strength of the Mexican economy. The tourist and construction industries are booming, which is attracting workers to Puerto Vallarta from all over Mexico. Unemployment is well below 3 percent, and a strong middle class is emerging. "They are becoming a much stronger factor in the local housing market and are helping to drive the overall real estate business," Charlie maintains. "Buyers with large disposable income from Mexico's large inland cities like Mexico City, and especially Guadalajara, because it is less than five hours from

PV by automobile, have become a growing market for home sales in Puerto Vallarta."

Condos are still the most popular form of housing purchased by Americans and Canadians, Charlie explains. "They're easy to take care of, someone is always there taking care of the property, and security is good. Condos are a real no-fuss, turnkey environment. The downside is that you have lots of neighbors and have to deal with condo associations. Houses, on the other hand, are very private and are yours to do with as you please. The downside to houses is that you have to do everything yourself, which can sometimes be a challenge, especially when you are new to the ways and customs of Mexico. If you are a part-time resident, it's best to pay someone to either stay at or watch your home. Most of the larger homes in Vallarta have service worker accommodations that allow a caretaker, housekeeper, and/or handyman to live at the house. Also, a number of property management firms have sprung up over the last few years to provide these services to homeowners, both condo and house owners."

As the baby boomer wave begins washing on shore, real estate firms in Vallarta are springing up like mushrooms, but Charlie cautions that buyers should carefully review each firm's capabilities. "The smaller firms tend to be more oriented toward buyers and not carry that many for sale listings, while the larger companies, like Coldwell Banker, do both. Coldwell Banker usually has over a hundred for sale listings at any given time. The Internet, also, has really changed how we and other real estate firms do business. Most people do their homework on the various real estate company Web sites as well as the Puerto Vallarta multi-listing site (http://www.mlsvallarta.com). By the time they hit the ground, they've selected an agent and have a good idea of what they want and where they want it."

Agents have to work a little harder in PV, Charlie thinks, because there is no lockbox system in Vallarta as there is in the U.S. and Canada. That means real estate agents have to coordinate showings when the house is available to be seen. For someone thinking about a purchase in PV, planning and coordination are essential in optimizing the time spent evaluating homes.

Charlie now lives in an apartment in the Versalles neighborhood, which is immediately east of the northern hotel zone. "I can smell the ocean from my apartment. I like it here because it's very quiet, centrally located, there are lots of nice people as neighbors, and we are situated among many large homes with far fewer apartments and condos. Quite a few Americans and Canadians live in Versalles, especially those looking for a large house with a pool and room for animals. As much as I like living her, I've been diligently saving my pennies and am now shopping for my own home."

Involvement in his local community is a big part of Charlie's life in Vallarta. "Since my girlfriend is Mexican and I speak the language fluently, I have many Mexican friends. My social life very much revolves around family gatherings, fiestas, and other local events. I've even had a chance to sample grasshoppers as a delicacy, at least once, anyway! I love this town, especially the people. It can be the most beautiful place in the world, but if the people aren't nice, you aren't going to like it. Fortunately for me, the people here are so warm and genuine and remarkably hopeful."

"The really cool thing, though, about living in Vallarta is the number of simple things that you can do, like watching a sunset or walking on the beach in the moonlight or watching the whales in the bay," Charlie muses. "God really did a good job with this place." He also scuba dives, so he loves the proximity to great diving locations like the underwater preserve at

Los Arcos, where divers can explore a thousand-foot wall. The Marietta Islands located at the mouth of the bay is another outstanding diving location with many caverns to explore and a terrific variety of fish. Majahuitas on the southern shore of the bay is another of Charlie's excellent diving locations, with its small but beautiful coral. Charlie, a history buff, explains that the bay itself is very deep, which is why it was a deep-water anchorage for the Spanish as well as pirates. The ships were used to transport gold and silver from San Sebastian del Oeste back to Spain. "I've always loved history, and this area is perfect for a history lover."

Charlie is a man of many interests and takes full advantage of the wide range of activities available in PV and the surrounding area. He is learning how to play the guitar and has found a great place in the north bay beach town La Cruz de Huanacaxtle that gives aspiring musicians the chance to play music with others three nights a week. "The Bucerias and La Cruz areas on the north shore have a lot of expat's living there," he says. "Philo's is the place, and Philo is a musician who understands musicians and tries to help them. He also has a small studio that he uses to help all of us aspiring musicians. He also puts on one of the best Thanksgiving dinners in the area. Philo supplies the turkeys, and you bring a side dish that is enough for six people. It's basically a potluck dinner. It's a great way to meet people and have some inexpensive fun."

Besides jamming in La Cruz, Charlie also is involved with the Toys for Tots charity program, which Coldwell Banker sponsors. He participates in all of the Toys for Tots events, like the golf tournament and an annual dinner. "I think the most fun of all is the King's Day event," he says. "On January 6, which is the King's Day holiday in Mexico when traditionally Christmas toys are given to the children, we go to schools in the middle of nowhere to give out toys. To see the look on a child's face when you give that child a gift is incredible."

After living in Vallarta for fourteen years, Charlie agrees that the cost of living has risen steadily and is not cheap. "After all, this is an international resort city. Food prices are similar to those back home, and the better restaurants are also comparably priced to comparative restaurants in the U.S. and Canada. But, luckily, we have a wide assortment of restaurants to match most pocket books. If you're willing to drive to a place like Rincon de Guayabitos, north of the city on the Pacific coast about an hour by car, you can get a fabulous seafood dinner at a beachfront restaurant for about seven dollars. I think it is a beautiful, charming, friendly, and inexpensive dining experience, and very good. You have to make an effort to find these places, but the search is very rewarding."

One thing that is cheaper in Mexico is gasoline, Charlie feels. Mexico is oil self-sufficient and not dependent on OPEC. The government-owned monopoly oil company sells through its chain of Pemex gas stations. A gallon of premium gas runs about 15 percent cheaper than a gallon of premium gas in the U.S. "Don't forget to tip the service attendant," Charlie reminds. "Wages are low in Mexico, and service workers depend upon their tips."

Moving to Vallarta has brought baby boomer Charlie Rondot the good life, and he is living every moment of it. He worries, though, that too much of a good thing may not be a good thing. "The booming growth of the last several years has brought some problems that we haven't had before. Traffic has grown not only with the building boom, but also with the changes several years ago in Mexican banking practices that now allow for new car financing. Banks had been very wary of extending credit for some years after the 1995 financial crisis in Mexico. Before the easing of credit over the last several years, those who owned cars drove mainly older used cars, but now it seems like everyone on the road has a new car. My job requires a lot of traveling around the bay, and I've really noticed the change in traffic congestion. Parking downtown is also a problem, even with the new parking garages. But, hey, let's face it. This isn't a small town anymore; it's rapidly evolving into a large, modern city."

The city may be booming and the traffic getting worse, but Charlie thinks old realities like cultural differences are often more worrisome for newcomers. "One of the hardest things for Americans and Canadians to get comfortable with when they move to PV is the cultural differences in how work gets done. Northerners are used to a much faster pace with an emphasis on efficiency. If you try to transfer that concept to Vallarta or anywhere in Mexico, or Latin America for that matter, you will be a very frustrated person. Business and social affairs are conducted at a far more leisurely pace. My advice is to just relax and enjoy the change. It will probably be good for your blood pressure. Thankfully, most people who move here are looking for a slower pace of life. It is an adjustment, though. Those who can't adjust usually return to their previous life fairly quickly. For me, I love it. I was looking for a place where I could turn down the volume, and Vallarta was it."

Keeping the volume turned down, as many have discovered, is literally much more of a problem in Mexico, but it serves Charlie well as an excellent metaphor for his life in paradise.

CHAPTER SIX

KATY OCHOA

Divorced
San Francisco, California
President, Playa del Sol Corporation

"I actually cried for a year when we moved to Puerto
Vallarta. I really didn't like it."

Katy Ochoa is truly a baby boomer adventurer. She first
tasted the pleasures of Mexico at twenty-five and, twenty-one
years later, is still relishing her adventures in paradise. The
forty-six-year-old was born in San Francisco as a sixth generation Californian to a mother who died when Katy was still very
young and a father who was a well-known and successful attorney. The family—including a brother and two half-sisters—
lived in the upscale community of Piedmont in the Oakland
Hills and then moved to the equally upscale town of Tiburon,
across the bay from San Francisco. Katy left high school when
she was seventeen to begin a life odyssey that would end—at
least for now—in Puerto Vallarta.

While she was still in her teens, Katy left the Bay Area
to ski, first in Lake Tahoe and then in Aspen. After the skiing
season was over in Aspen, Katy returned to California, where
she enrolled at Sonoma State University for three semesters and

worked at her father's Tiburon law office. She met her artist husband during that time, and the two of them decided to move to Hawaii. They were living on the big island of Hawaii for a little over a year when Katy became pregnant with their first child, a boy. The couple returned to San Francisco for the birth of the baby, which was followed by another son a few years later. But after five years of marriage, John and Katy called it quits and divorced.

Two years after her divorce at the age of twenty-five, Katy sold everything she had and took her two boys to Zihuatanejo to sort things out under the benevolent Mexican sun. Her only previous exposure to Mexico prior to moving to Zihuatanejo had been family trips to Mexico City and Cuernavaca when she was young. She had also spent a year in Spain with her father when she was just six years old. Remembrances of the culture and her positive childhood experiences in Mexico drew her back.

Katy had planned to stay in Zihuatanejo for only three months and had rented an apartment for just that length of time. Her sons were a year and a half and four years old at the time and were thoroughly enjoying the warm sands and water of Playa La Ropa. Katy had not planned to live in Mexico beyond the three months, viewing the trip as a break in her life to reassess things.

The warm tropical nights intervened, though, and Katy met and fell in love with Sam Ochoa, who was a waiter at the local Carlos and Charlie's restaurant. They remained in Zihuatanejo for a year and then returned to San Francisco, but they discovered that making a living there wasn't all that easy. After the birth of their daughter, they returned to Guadalajara where Sam was offered a job with the same restaurant chain he had worked for in Zihuatanejo. Unfortunately, Mexico's economic crisis of 1995 occurred just as he took the new job, and he was soon laid off.

The Mexican economy was in shambles at that time, which forced the family to move from more expensive Guadalajara to a small town on the southern Jalisco coast called Melaque, where they rented a modest palapa house on the beach for eighty dollars a month. Desperate for money, Sam contacted the people he had worked for in San Francisco, who recognized the family's dire money problems and flew him back to the Bay Area to work for them.

Meanwhile, Katy and the kids remained in the coastal village but had no money other than five pesos. Before Sam left, though, he went to the local stores and asked them to extend credit to Katy and look out for her and the kids until he could start sending money, which they all gladly did. "To this day, I can still drive through that town, stop at the gas station, and have someone come up to me and say hello," Katy fondly remembers. "I stayed there for months in that little palm-thatched place with those wonderful people. It was lovely living on the beach, a truly no-stress place to live."

Sam returned in 1997 and fortunately found work again at Carlos and Charlie's, this time in the large west coast port city of Manzanillo, a short drive south of Melaque.

"After we moved to Manzanillo, I found work with a woman who lived in an exclusive residential area around the famous Las Hadas hotel," Katy says. "She wanted to organize high-end executive sports tours for people who stayed at the properties she owned in that area, kind of an earlier version of what Vallarta Adventures is now. She paid me the first year to do research by driving to every possible location for the sports tours in the state of Colima. My research was good because I got maps from the Mexican census bureau, which has the most detailed maps of the country. They map every little lane and cow path where people live, not just existing highways. I also guided a number of the executive tours. The job was also great because the woman had two beautiful homes in La Punta, the peninsula area where Las Hadas is located. She let us live in one of them for a while. We felt like we were living in that old television show, *The Beverly Hillbillies*."

Soon afterward, though, Katy and Sam found a house to purchase on a hill with a nice view of the ocean. Katy started a new job—as the administrator of a school that taught English—and soon discovered that administration was her true calling. She liked it and was very good at it. She also taught English at the school to wealthy Mexican families in Manzanillo, usually in small groups with no more than four people. "I worked with a lovely group of people, and we had a great time. I handled the overall administration as well as hiring all of the teachers, none of them, by the way, run of the mill. I had a surfer, a sexy girl, and an engineer, a real mix of people. The school did very well because it appealed to wealthy families that enrolled all members of the family. The girls liked the surfer guy, the guys liked the sexy girl, and so forth. It's called marketing, I believe."

Their life changed again when Sam's company gave him an opportunity to open a restaurant in Cabo San Lucas, the fast-growing resort area in Baja Sur. He was sent to Cancun for training, but a hurricane in Cabo changed Sam's plans. Since he was trained by that time for restaurant management, the company asked him to choose between restaurants in Cancun and Puerto Vallarta. He chose PV because they were going to open a new Señor Frog's, and he wanted to be part of that operation.

At the same time, Katy was offered a job as the administrator of the English school in Puerto Vallarta, which was part of the same chain of schools as the one she worked for in Manzanillo. Katy soon discovered that the school in Vallarta had many problems, so she had to put in long hours to turn it around. She commuted from Manzanillo to PV for months before she and the kids finally moved to Vallarta for good in 1999. She worked weekends in PV and continued weekday work at the school in Manzanillo. Katy usually took the four-hour bus ride to PV, leaving late Friday night and returning late Sunday night, but sometimes she would drive and find herself always stopped at the same military checkpoint on Highway 200, the main highway between Manzanillo and Puerto Vallarta. "The commandant would always ask why I was driving this highway alone late at night. He was worried about me and always gave me the same message to tell Sam: 'You tell your husband that a pretty young girl shouldn't be driving the highways of Mexico in the middle of the night.' I was touched by his caring and became friends with the commandant, and although he gave me the same lecture each time, I didn't stop making that trip."

When the kids got out of school, they moved to Vallarta to rejoin Sam. They found it was very difficult to find good housing in Vallarta, though. "Puerto Vallarta was really inhospitable to families at that time. We were a family that traveled through Mexico with three kids and three large dogs and never had a problem until we moved to PV. At one point, we had to get an attorney involved because Sam went to see a house and was told that they would rent it to him. But when all of us showed up to sign the contract, they tried to back out of it. It was very difficult around 2000 because there was not a lot of reasonably priced housing for rent that had good schools in the neighborhood and would take three kids and dogs."

Their first place in Vallarta was an apartment on the south side of the Cuale River. "It was good that it wasn't expensive because we were sending the kids to private schools and needed the extra money for tuition. In Mexico, it's always the best option to send your kids to private schools to ensure they receive the best education."

After renting for a while, the family decided to buy a home in the Cinco de Diciembre neighborhood, in the northern part of the downtown area. "It was ugly, but it was ours," Katy laughs. "After we moved in I started working at a clothing store for women on Olas Altas on the south side of Vallarta that imported goods from Indonesia. I managed the business for the owners, who also owned two other stores in town and lived in Yelapa. I also started getting other work as I began to meet more people who discovered that I was both bilingual and had lots of administrative experience."

Katy worked for the clothing store on Olas Altas for several years before deciding to start her own business. She opened another retail store for women that featured imported goods. The new store—Eclipse—was located in the center of the city, but it did poorly, mainly because of its location on a side street. Thankfully, she was still doing the books for several other companies, so her income continued.

When Eclipse failed after a year and a half of long hours and hard work, Katy took a break. By that time the family was renting a house in Versalles east of the hotel zone and renting out their place in Cinco de Diciembre. Change continued for Katy when the boys left to live with their dad in San Francisco so they could complete high school and go on to college.

After a period of recuperation, Katy eased back into work, taking a job with a local art gallery where she worked in the afternoon. Following that, she took another low-stress job at a local jewelry store, which allowed her to work a few hours in the evening and have the rest of the day off. While working there, she bumped into an old friend who told her there was a position open at Playa del Sol Corporation she might be interested in.

Katy not only got the job, but she shot to the top of the corporation in just two years. "I started working for them in 2003 in member services. At the time I started, Playa del Sol had one hotel on Playa Los Muertos, and they were building a large hotel in Nuevo Vallarta. They were basically in the time-share business. After I cleaned up member services, I took over the inventory job. In a very short period of time, I became the corporation's vice president in charge of operations and quality of the hotels. Then, in 2005, Playa del Sol promoted me to president of the corporation."

Katy explains that the corporation now has expanded to include several properties. "We have the original Playa del Sol property, a new resort in Nuevo Vallarta, and properties in Cabo San Lucas and Cancun. We also purchased Costa Vida on the south shore and renamed it Playa del Sol."

She hires only Mexican employees at Playa del Sol because she believes they are hard workers and do a terrific job. "Foreigners never pass my hiring filter because they come with a more relaxed attitude, knowing that they are in a laid-back, beautiful resort town. They just don't put in the hours we require. Another thing I find is a lack of excellence in Vallarta when it comes to workers. If you're even a little bit better than average, you can really shine here. The other thing is this is Mexico, and you need to speak the language. I don't hire anyone who doesn't speak Spanish. I also don't generally hang out with people who don't speak Spanish. When we lived in Guadalajara, all the foreign women I hung out with spoke perfect Spanish. When I got to Vallarta, no one spoke Spanish."

Her own theory is that many people who move to Vallarta are not that social and therefore don't see a need to become fluent in Spanish. Katy doesn't understand why anyone would want to move to a country where they can't speak the language. "Mexico is a negotiator's paradise," she says. "Everything about this culture is a negotiation. One of the reasons why I have my job is that I grew up in this culture, am fluent in Spanish, and I'm a good negotiator."

Katy now has a home in the Marina area and likes the quiet neighborhood she lives in. She also likes the people she works with and very much likes her job. "Working at Playa del Sol is what I really like about Vallarta. I'm in charge of 550 people and am proud of helping make my company one of the best places to work in PV. When I took this job a few years ago, our turnover was nearly 55 percent, and now it is down to just 3 percent." She is usually at her desk very early in the morning, but she makes it a point to go home by late afternoon each day to spend quality time with her daughter.

Katy's daughter still lives at home and attends a private school. She has one year left to graduation and has been offered a scholarship to attend one of the most prestigious technical universities in Mexico, located in Monterrey.

Education is always on Katy's mind. One of the big negatives Katy points out about Vallarta is the inattention paid to education by the local business community. "You're shooting yourself in the foot by not doing it," Katy complains. "Schools are not that good in Vallarta, so I pay the tuition for three girls to go to private schools. I think more hotels and other businesses should be either sponsoring kids in private schools or working to improve the public schools. Playa del Sol has set up a scholarship program to help improve education here. We are the only company doing it, which is sad and, frankly, poor business for a community that depends on a better educated work force. Finding qualified people, especially at the mid-range management level, is very difficult."

Life in PV generally is good for Katy, but she has lingering doubts about Vallarta's status as a paradise. "I actually cried for a year when we moved to Puerto Vallarta," she admits. "I really didn't like it. I loved all of my other Mexican experiences, but moving to Vallarta was like coming back to what I felt were the rules of the states, not the freedom I felt in other areas of Mexico. Vallarta is an American version of Mexico, an international resort city that just happens to be in Mexico. When we first moved here, it also seemed that everybody looked out only for them in a way that was completely foreign to my Mexican experience. I can see why now. In Vallarta, with its large base of expats and tourists, it's still mostly about the money. There are good jobs and lots of opportunities here because Vallarta is the best place to work in Mexico. Our pay scales are so much higher than the rest of the country."

Now that she has an executive-level job and makes a lot more money, Katy is much happier living in Vallarta, but she still misses the warmth of the families and friends she had while living in other areas of Mexico. She also laments the fact that she and her friends in Vallarta are all too busy to do the simple things in life she misses from her past. "Going to the beach was a part of my life for a very long time, but in Vallarta it is not," Katy regretfully says. "I did a lot of ocean swimming, and the beach was an integral part of our life. Not anymore, though. We live right next to the beautiful Bay of Banderas, but everyone seems to be too busy to enjoy it. Vallarta is a lovely place to retire, but right now I'm working."

CHAPTER SEVEN

BOBBIE SNYDER

Married
Vancouver, Washington
Partner, Real Estate Vallarta & Beyond

BILL SNYDER

Married
Vancouver, Washington
Retired

"The fact is that everybody comes here with the expectation this is Mexico, but they want to change it to be like home."

Bobbie and Bill Snyder are early retirees who pulsate with energy, fed by a tropical climate that allows them access to the outdoors every day of the year. They fled the cold and windy winters of the Pacific Northwest nine years ago and have never looked back. Like their baby boomer cohorts, Bobbie and Bill were up for an adventure and seeking a sun-soaked paradise south of the border. They found it in Puerto Vallarta.

At sixty-three, Bill Snyder is a little older than the age-defined baby boomer. He was born and raised in Vancouver, Washington, and lived in that area his entire life prior to coming to Puerto Vallarta. His father was a farmer, so Bill grew up knowing the value of hard work. After Bill graduated from the University of Oregon with a bachelor's degree in accounting and business management, he returned to Vancouver and worked for several companies doing financial work. In 1976, a friend who attended the same church that he did told him of a business opportunity to purchase the Anderson Glass company, an existing firm that was in the construction business, selling glass and structural products.

Bill sold his business in 1996 and retired at the young age of fifty-one. He had worked hard all of his life; in fact, he had a checking account when he was eleven years old and was paying into Social Security by the time he was fourteen. His parents taught him about the value of hard work and responsibility, and it paid off for him later in life.

Bobbie was born in Seattle at the beginning of the baby boomer wave in 1946, but she doesn't remember much about the city because her family moved to Hawaii when she was very young. She was raised on the windward side of Oahu in a small town called Kailua. At that time, Hawaii was still a territory and not a state. She recalls growing up in an idyllic environment, similar to what she found years later in Vallarta. "We grew up not wearing shoes, spending most of our time at the beach, and enjoying the beauty and sunshine of Hawaii, much of what I love about PV now," Bobbie says.

Bobbie moved to Vancouver, Washington, in the mid-1980s because she had a friend there who kept raving about it. Her daughter was about ready to go to college, and her son was in ninth grade at that time. She got a job in the construction industry and worked in that business for about four years. But when her son graduated from high school and was ready to go to college, she also decided to go, while continuing to work full-time. The only class she could fit into her busy schedule was real estate, and she enjoyed it so much that after three months of school Bobbie decided to become a real estate agent. She was successful from the very beginning of her real estate career and was a top seller in the Portland-Vancouver area for nine years. Bobbie was on the top of her game just at the time Bill decided to take early retirement. She had her own radio talk show on real estate and was one of the top producers in the area. She wasn't sure she was ready for retirement.

When Bill retired, he and Bobbie moved to a new home they had built on the Long Beach peninsula, situated at the mouth of the Columbia River. They lasted just one year at their retirement place, driven south by too much wind and rain. "I refused to spend another winter at Long Beach and told Bill to get me out of here," Bobbie laughs. Bill had purchased four lots as investments and built what they initially thought was just going to be a beach house, but turned into, at least for a year, their first retirement home. "We just couldn't survive the winters," says Bill. "The first January we spent there, it rained twenty-eight days. Bobbie was used to the weather in Hawaii and needed the sun and warmth."

Bill had visited Puerto Vallarta several times, but Bobbie had never been. PV was on Bill's retirement short list of resort areas on Mexico's west coast, based on the positive experiences he had in PV on vacation. He loved the weather, the beaches, the warm bay water, and especially the prospects of getting out on the bay for some good fishing. So, Bill and Bobbie got in their car and headed south of the border for a five-month car trip to Mexico to look for a new, sunnier retirement spot.

The couple's adventure took them down the west coast of Oregon and California to Mexico and then followed the western coast of mainland Mexico all the way down to Acapulco, looking for the ideal place to buy or build a house.

As they wound their way down the serpentine Mexican coast, they stopped first in the Guaymas and San Carlos area to look at real estate and then drove on to Los Mochis, but the desert-like topography north of Mazatlan did not appeal to them. "We aren't desert people; we like it more tropical," Bill explains. They pressed on down the coast to Mazatlan, Puerto Vallarta, then Zihuatanejo, and finally to Acapulco, stopping along the highway to check out all of the retirement possibilities.

For the most part, their five-month tour of coastal cities was uneventful, but Bobbie remembers they were scared once during the trip. "We were warned to watch out for bandits in the mountains from Acapulco north. Driving the two-lane road with many hairpin turns was scary enough, but then we came around a blind turn, and a rope went up across the road, blocking our vehicle. We thought it was bandits for sure, but it turned out to be local villagers trying to raise money for a young girl's *quincinera*!" They gladly contributed, the rope was lifted, and they were once again on their way.

The couple decided Vallarta was the place for them after considering several different locations. They found a lot on a canal in Nuevo Vallarta with a boat dock and a sea wall that would allow Bill to jump in a boat and get out on to the bay with ease. They looked at each other and grinned. This was their place.

Bill and Bobbie liquidated most of their holdings in the U.S. and decided to live full-time in Mexico. They started construction on their home in Nuevo Vallarta in 1999 and were one of the first to build in that area. It took sixteen months to construct the house, based on Bobbie's own design with the help of an architect. In building the house, they learned a very important cultural lesson: Mexican people have a difficult time saying no. Bobbie sighs, "It would have been much easier building the house if we had lived here first for a few years to better understand the culture and how business is done before plunging in and building a home."

They were very comfortable with the real estate agent who worked with them on the sale of the property, but they discovered many bumps along the road in building their five thousand square foot villa with five bedrooms and eight baths on two floors.

First, Bobbie and Bill hired an architect/contractor to build their home, but they discovered later that he didn't understand all the terms of the contract he signed. "He was over his head, but we didn't know it," Bill confesses. "We fulfilled our part of the contract, but he didn't fulfill his. He delivered a shell of a house after we had given him money above what the contract stipulated. We had to put additional money into the house to finish it. The architect/contractor then came back a year after the house was finished and demanded that we pay him more money. Of course, we refused and were served with a lawsuit." Bobbie and Bill discovered that in Mexico it's often more about who you know and who has the best story to tell than the actual facts of the situation. They won their first and second court cases after six years of litigation. The architect/contractor has now appealed the ruling to the highest court, which could take up to two more years. After upwards of $30,000 in legal costs, Bobbie and Bill still cannot see the light at the end of the tunnel.

Now, completely settled in her new home on the canals of Nuevo Vallarta, Bobbie likes the similarities to Hawaii, including the diverse and rich mix of people found in both places. "What's wonderful about both Hawaii and Mexico is that everybody gets along and is friendly. In the states, everybody is behind closed doors. You don't know your neighbor down the street. Here, we find it easy to meet people because everyone is friendly."

Bobbie and Bill are most definitely extroverted, very friendly people. They introduce themselves often to people on the street and in restaurants and just chat with them. They try to engage people wherever they go. "We met very good friends while out bike riding," Bill says. "We also strike up conversations on the buses to and from our home in Nuevo Vallarta. It's a lot of fun to meet new people this way." The language has not been a barrier for the couple, though. They've been taking Spanish lessons on and off ever since they moved to Mexico to help them communicate better, but they admit they still have some trouble speaking Spanish.

As extroverted as they are, Bobbie and Bill don't belong to the large International Friendship Club (IFC) in PV or any other expat organization, although Bobbie says she is the IFC's "go to" person in Nuevo Vallarta. That means she finds homes on the north shore for inclusion in the club's home show program, which features guided tours of some of Vallarta's most glamorous homes.

But being the "go to" person for the IFC still wasn't enough for the vivacious and pulsating Bobbie. She decided she was too active a person to retire full-time, so she went back to real estate in 2004, working with two different companies before starting her own firm. Being a true baby boomer adventurer, Bobbie candidly says she got bored. "You can only sit in the sun so many hours and read so many books. I decided to go back to what I do best, and that's selling real estate." Her new company—Real Estate Vallarta & Beyond—is a partnership with two other women, both Mexican.

Bill, on the other hand, is enjoying his retirement. He fishes a couple of times a week, at least. He has a twenty-eight-foot fishing boat that was made just up the coast in Mazatlan. His favorite fishing holes are the Marietta Islands west of Punta de Mita and off the coast of Sayulita, just north of Punta de Mita. "I don't belong to the Nuevo Vallarta Yacht Club, but I do participate in some of their activities," Bill says. "They have what they call their 'February Fishing Frenzy,' which is a very fun competition I take part in. We have to be back at the club by four in the afternoon each day during the competition to register our catch, and then we sit down at six for a fresh-catch fish dinner. Prizes are awarded, and everyone has a great time. I catch dorado, mahimahi, yellow fin tuna, and other fish in the tuna family."

Even living a half hour or so north of Puerto Vallarta, the couple makes it a point to get into the city as often as they can. When they make the fifteen-mile trip into Vallarta from their home, they frequently like to visit the city's wide range of art galleries. They know a lot of the gallery owners and have developed a large art collection. "We have a vehicle that we can take into Puerto Vallarta, but often we take public transportation," Bill explains. "We can get picked up and dropped off by the bus right in front of our house. For a few dollars, we can go anywhere in Vallarta on the public bus system. It's very efficient, inexpensive, and buses run all of the time."

It's also less nerve-wracking for the couple. "Big changes have occurred in Vallarta; it's no longer a sleepy little town," Bill confesses. "It's a bustling, busy, dusty, car-inundated city in perpetual construction mode. Parking has become horrendous, which makes riding the buses, of course, look even better. With the change in bank lending practices here, everyone wants a new car. New auto dealerships have sprouted seemingly everywhere. I think they put up the new Toyota dealership north of the airport in about three months. And, I don't think, by the way, that a *topes* is a traffic solution. Those speed bumps are ubiquitous; you seemingly can't drive anywhere without having to slow down for them. But they're not the solution to every traffic problem. What they really need to do is construct cloverleaf overpasses and develop the infrastructure to carry the load, and that's not happening right now, as far as I can see."

When the couple first moved to the Bay of Banderas, the main road from Nuevo Vallarta to Puerto Vallarta was then a two-lane road, but it now has been expanded to four lanes. "We were the only American couple present when Mexico's then president Vicente Fox came to inaugurate the new bridge and highway over the Ameca River," Bill recalls. "There were three or four hundred people at the ceremony, but Fox came over to speak with us, which greatly impressed Bobbie and me. We were laughing because he inaugurated the bridge that day but would not inaugurate the new highway because only two of the four lanes had been completed. He told the local officials to call him when the other two lanes were done, and he would come back and officially inaugurate the highway at that time. And he did."

The new highway has been open for just a few years now, but it's already often at capacity, the result of planned new developments along the north shore of the bay and the western coast of the state of Nayarit. Mexico's National Tourism Development Foundation (FONATUR), the same government agency that developed Cancun and Ixtapa, is a prime developer of the Riviera Nayarit. When completed, FONATUR's development will stretch from the town of Litibu—sandwiched between Punta de Mita and Sayulita—to El Capomo, just south of Las Varas on the south coast of the state of Nayarit. By 2020, FONATUR claims there will be nearly fifteen thousand additional rooms for tourist and residential lodging, which should attract an additional one million tourists each year.

More development doesn't really bother Bobbie and Bill, though. Vallarta is their paradise, and they love it. "Weather is without question the number one reason we are living here," Bill says. "The beauty of living in Vallarta is that inside living is the same as outside living. We spend half our time on the patio outside by the pool and the boat dock."

With Bobbie running her own business now, Bill does most of the cooking and the shopping. The best thing he likes about grocery shopping in PV is the fresh tree- or vine-ripened produce. "The fruits and vegetables are better than anything you can buy in the states," Bill concludes. "We stay away from the snack foods and other junk, except for the local ice cream, which is awesome." Bill also catches a lot of fish each week, which becomes the protein for most meals. They eat healthy food, and that makes them feel better and saves them money.

Eating healthy helps them stay healthy, also. Bobbie especially likes the more natural approach to health care in Vallarta. She had an ultrasound done locally, which revealed gallstones. The doctor told her not to let them operate on her in the States to remove the stones. Instead, the doctor recommended that for nine days she take olive oil and squeezed lime juice every morning, eat a green apple at night, and lie on her left side when she slept. She did, and the problem went away. For Mexican doctors, she says, surgery is the last resort.

With a large house and busy lives, the couple is fortunate to have two local people work for them full-time as maid and handyman. They have become very close to their employees and now pay the yearly tuition for their two kids—ages eight and five—to attend a K–12 bilingual school located near the PV airport. They also funded an Olympic-size swimming pool for Colegio Mexico-Americano, which now has the second best swimmer in all of Mexico who is representing Mexico in the 2008 Olympics in Beijing, China.

After nine years of living in Paradise, Bobbie and Bill have found a home for life. "Besides the great weather every day, we love the fact that local people will always stop and talk with you," Bobbie enthuses. "That doesn't happen very often where we came from. People there tend to look down when they walk by you. Here, everybody looks up and says *hola*, and you can strike up a conversation with a total stranger, if you like. The people are very open and more than willing to help you."

"We're here for the duration," Bobbie proclaims, "even with all of the growth and changes we have seen. The fact is that everybody comes here with the expectation this is Mexico, but they want to change it to be like home. They want to bring certain things with them so that life is easier and more familiar for them. In many respects, Vallarta is becoming more and more like the States or Canada, with Home Depot, Sam's, Wal-Mart, Costco, and the enclosed malls. It didn't exist before, and that's why people would come here. That's a big reason why we came here. Now, they could be anywhere. It's a big international resort city, not the charming, small town we once knew. I don't think it's necessarily a negative, it's just what happens when growth comes to stay."

CHAPTER EIGHT

LEN GREENOUGH

Committed Partner
Atlanta, Georgia
Owner/Operator Blu Salon

LARRY SHELDON

Committed Partner
Atlanta, Georgia
Semi-Retired

"I have great faith in the Mexican people. Unfortunately,
though, I think a lot of the people who move here
come with the assumption that the Mexican people
don't know anything. The Mexican people know a lot.
They're playing catch-up, but things are improving."

Len Greenough and Larry Sheldon bracket the baby boom
generation in age, but are as harmonious with the cohort's
dreams and desires as any full-fledged boomer. The two have
quickly established themselves as Vallarta expat and gay community leaders.

Larry was born in the little town of McAllen, Texas, in 1939, just seven miles from the Mexican border. He left there when he was five and grew up in Smithvale in central Texas, about forty miles south of Austin. Larry was an only child raised by his mother and his grandparents. He graduated from Baylor University in Waco, Texas, with a liberal arts degree before he "escaped" the state of Texas by joining the U.S. Navy. As a naval officer, Larry spent most of his time on the admiral's flagship in the Mediterranean. When he exited the navy, Larry joined IBM at a time when they seemingly couldn't hire enough people. He worked for IBM for thirty years, mainly in education and training in Heidelberg, Germany; Montreal, Canada; and other far-flung global locations before finally settling in Atlanta, Georgia. Larry retired early from IBM, but he kept working in Atlanta as a training consultant, specializing in organizational development and leadership prior to moving to PV.

Larry's life partner Len also was a Texas boy. Born just two years after the baby boom officially ended, Len, like Larry, shares their values. Len's father was a Canadian Air Force pilot, so he dutifully moved every two or three years with his parents, two younger brothers, and a sister. He has lived all over the United States and Canada and is a citizen of both countries. When he grew up, Len moved to Vancouver, Canada, and opened a men's boutique clothing store, although he realized after a few years he was definitely a warm weather person, and Vancouver's cool, drizzly weather was clearly not the place for him. After a few bottles of wine one night, he got out a map of the U.S., shut his eyes, and decided to move to the area his finger landed on. Atlanta, Georgia, was the spot. One month later, Len found himself in the Georgia capital, alone and with no friends. But the one key thing he had learned as an air force "brat" helped him make his transition to Atlanta much easier: flexibility. Moving

every two or three years made making deep friendships difficult for Len, but the experience of moving often also equipped
him with the ability to make changes easily and start fresh in
each new place. The warmth of Atlanta agreed with Len, who
lived there for eighteen years and never had an itch to move
anywhere else. He had finally found a place to call home, or so
he thought.

In Atlanta, Len decided to try his hand as a hair stylist.
"I had been doing 'kitchen hair' since I was nine or ten years
old, non-professional work for friends and family," Len recalls.
"After I moved to Atlanta, I became one of the oldest living
beauty school students when I enrolled in my thirties. It took
me nine months and fifteen hundred hours of training to get
through that school. I never really liked the classroom work,
but I discovered that this was something I really wanted to do.
After graduation, I got a job working at the salon in the Ritz-
Carlton hotel in Atlanta. When I started working there, they
told me to forget everything I learned in beauty school because
now I was going to really learn how to cut hair. I cut hair at the
Ritz for three years, just prior to moving to Vallarta. I learned
a lot. One thing I learned was that southern women take their
beauty very seriously. There is an old saying in the beauty
business—at least in the South—'The higher the hair, the closer
to God.' I had such great fun for those three years at the Ritz.
It was the perfect blend of beautiful women and their psychotic
hair stylists."

Len and Larry like to tell people they moved to Vallarta the
day after George Bush was reelected president of the United
States in 2004. It was symbolic for them, but in actuality, they
had planned to make the move prior to what they call "that
dark day." They had been living in Vallarta six months every
year for several years prior to their full-time move. They had
planned to come down for six months once again, but after

they were in PV for a while, they looked at each other and asked: "Why should we go back to Atlanta?" Neither had a good answer, so they decided to live full-time in Puerto Vallarta. That's when Len decided to open his own salon, and the couple committed to make a permanent life in PV.

Larry had been coming to Puerto Vallarta since 1996 and, like so many people before him, fell in love the first time he laid eyes on the place. "I was here a week, and by the end of that week, I owned a time-share at the Sheraton, that's how much I knew I loved the town," Larry remembers. "Then I met Len in Atlanta, and we started dating and taking trips together. I asked him to come to PV with me in 1998. When he set foot on this sandy soil, he fell in love instantly. We were walking into town from the Sheraton along the beach, and I think it was just near the Bonaventura when I proposed to him. He accepted, and we decided right there on that beach by the Bay of Banderas that we would go back to Atlanta and do it right. We would have a formal commitment ceremony with a minister and all of our family and friends attending. Before we left PV, we went to the Sergio Bustamante gallery and bought our wedding rings."

The couple then started coming two or three times a year using their Sheraton time-share. In 2002, they bought a condominium in Amapas—a hillside neighborhood overlooking the south side of Vallarta and the bay—and started coming for six months at a time during the winter. During that period, Len would fly back and forth during the winter, working at a salon in Vallarta and also at the Ritz-Carlton, so he could take care of his Atlanta clients. When they would return to Atlanta for the summer, Len would do the same thing, except in reverse. It was physically trying, so Len and Larry made the decision to leave Atlanta behind and become full-time residents of Vallarta in 2004.

"We loved our little place in Amapas, our first condo," Larry exudes. "It had a great view of the bay and the city. You know, I think that's the way it happens to so many people. You start coming on trips, and then you start coming for a few months at a time, and before long you finally decide: Why go back?"

Len and Larry were in love with Puerto Vallarta's fabulous weather and the juxtaposition of the bay and the mountains. "It's so beautiful, so striking here," Len admires. "The bay itself is beautiful, and the town is so charming with its carefully preserved cobblestone streets and the new, beautiful Malecon that now winds along the bay for over two miles. It makes it so easy to just meander around town, and it's beautiful, too, with many original bronzes donated by famous Mexican sculptors placed all along the boardwalk."

PV reminded Larry a great deal of some locations in Europe he had visited during his IBM days. "As we sat in our new condo high on the hill above Vallarta and watched the sun go down and the lights twinkle on around the bay, it looked very much like Sorrento, Italy, or some other places I have been on the Mediterranean. Absolutely gorgeous."

Neither Len nor Larry had any second thoughts about moving to PV, but Len was concerned about learning Spanish. He didn't study a second language while in school and was worried that he wouldn't be able to work or communicate. Fortunately, he found that many people speak English in PV because of its dependence on American and Canadian tourism, so he has been able to live and communicate using "just enough" Spanish. But Len thinks that if you live here permanently, you should at least try to speak the language. "It's so funny when I see Americans raising their voices when speaking to the local people, as if by speaking English louder, somehow the language barrier would be transcended." Language is no longer a concern for Len since his comprehension of Spanish has improved. Larry, on the other hand, has taken classes locally and speaks Spanish very well. He took intensive classes at the University of Guadalajara extension program when he first arrived, but he admits that his Spanish has improved primarily by speaking it every day.

After making the move to full-time living in PV, one of Larry's initial concerns was medical care. "When we were coming here for six months at a time, it wasn't a big issue," he says. "I have my health insurance through the IBM retirement program, and we saw our doctors in Atlanta. When we started living here full-time, though, and began to use local providers we realized how fine they were. You can get some of the best medical care in the world here. You can't find hospitals north of the border that will give you the same kind of loving care that the Mexican doctors and nurses give you."

Len can attest to that. He had his appendix removed at San Javier Hospital, which is located across from the maritime terminal where the cruise ships dock. He says it was not only the cleanest hospital he had seen in his entire life, but he also feels that they handled his emergency appendectomy better than any hospital in the U.S. would have. "From the time I went to the doctor's office where my appendicitis was diagnosed until I was wheeled into the operating room, it was less than an hour and a half. If I had been in the States, I probably would have died. My appendix burst on the operating table. The admitting paperwork alone up north would have taken an hour and half." He was in the hospital for seven days to guard against infection and peritonitis. The entire bill with private room, excellent patient care, surgery, and drugs was less than fourteen thousand dollars.

Reflecting their baby boomer predilections, the couple found that not doing very much didn't suit them. "The funny thing about moving here was that we wanted to have less on our plates and enjoy life, but the irony is that after the first year we were down here, we had too much on our plates," Larry says. "We were so busy, all of the time. When we moved, it wasn't with the idea we were retiring, but rather relocating to a place we loved."

For Len it was a career move to open his own salon. A year after they arrived to live full-time in 2004, his salon Blu opened, a record time to open a business in Mexico considering the mountain of paper work they had faced. "Interestingly, there are some things you don't think of at all when moving here, which come to you as a shock once you arrive," Len explains. "Like dealing with government bureaucracy and opening a business here. The process is so different than what we are used to back home. You just have to take the time to learn your way around."

And learn they did. After Larry and Len signed the lease for Blu's space, which was designated specifically for a beauty salon, they discovered that it was not actually zoned for that use. "You can't take anything for granted," Len cautions. "You need to check everything, all the details. Luckily, we were able to circumvent that problem and move forward with construction." If that wasn't enough, Len's former employer in Vallarta filed a *demando*—a lawsuit under Mexico's Napoleonic code of law—against him for hiring one of Len's former co-workers at the other salon. The *demando* was filed with the Mexican immigration office and made nearly a dozen claims against Len. He had to spend time to disprove each one. It was a stressful three-month period for Len and Larry, considering that the real possibility existed that Len could be deported if any of the claims were proved. Finally, the *demando* was settled, but not until the police closed the new salon on the day of its grand opening. "You just don't know about these issues until you do it," Len sighs. "It's the difference between fully retiring here and wanting to be active and running a business."

And there is a big difference between those who fully retire and those who continue to work. "If you come down here with the idea that you are retired, you want to stay retired, you have enough money to stay retired, you don't want to do anything but wake up in the morning and go to the beach; if this is the retirement you want, then great, it's a piece of cake living in Vallarta," Larry says. "As long as you have money to sustain yourself, that's all Mexican immigration cares about, and no one bothers you. If you are like us, and most of the baby boomers, who either can't or don't want to retire, you have to be prepared for dealing with the local system. And that can be a challenge."

Their busy lives also impact the amount of time they have to participate in expat activities, particularly the plethora of charities. "We just finished a fund-raiser for women's heart health that was very successful," Larry notes. "However, success brings the opportunity to continue your success. We get calls all of the time asking us to run charity events for other groups. We would love to help, but there are just so many hours in a day, and we are both so busy with our jobs and lives, it's hard. We're not retired."

But all work spoils the boy, so Larry and Len carve out time for a social life, also. They do a lot of cooking at home and entertaining. They especially love going to local restaurants two or three times a week, unless there is a charity function they need to attend. "This is a very social town," Len says. "We do more in three months during high season here than we used to do in a year in Atlanta. Mexicans are very social people. They love to go out, have fiestas, and visit with their friends and family, and the expats follow suit. Everybody has parties and get-togethers. It used to be that most of the socialization was house parties, but with the rise in nonprofit events, that's capturing more and more of social time."

Although they loved their condo in Amapas, the couple
started looking for a new place to live right after Blu opened.
They had only a month to find a place because they had just
sold their condo and needed a place fast or soon would be living
in the salon. Their Amapas condo spoiled them with its view
and its layout, so they had certain prerequisites and high standards for a new space. First, they knew they wanted to live in
the hills south of Puerto Vallarta, which meant either Amapas
or Conchas Chinas. "We specifically wanted that view, both bay
and city," Larry remarks. "We also knew we wanted to live in
a condo. We had designed a house and were planning to build,
but fortunately we were able to get out of the deal. With running businesses and having very active lives, the responsibility
of having a house was not practical for us. We wanted a condo
where someone would take care of everything. We fortunately
found a place with a jaw-dropping view, great layout, and the
right price range. And the fact that it was a no-maintenance
condo made the purchase even better. We have marble floors,
granite countertops, stainless kitchen appliances, all top-notch
materials, appliances, and finishing, with a killer view. This
condo would cost at least three times as much as any ocean
view condo we could have bought in the States. We love it
here in Conchas Chinas, and the condo's thirty-five hundred
square feet of space and contemporary design gives us plenty
of room."

Although many expats view Puerto Vallarta's growth of the
last several years negatively, Len, as a business owner, thinks
development is positive for the city. "No city is ever ready for
the rapid growth that has taken place. They will always play
catch-up, but the catch-up has been well done. I like having
Starbucks here, not because I go to Starbucks, but it's just nice
to have for those expats and Mexicans who want that experience. They haven't built the Chili's restaurants, Sam's, Costco,

and other new retail stores for us expats. They're being built because the Mexican people want them, and the local population demographics can support them now."

Len has a very specific point of view on expats who move to Puerto Vallarta. "They should not complain about the traffic, cars, and the eighty cents to park per hour at the downtown garages. I just came back from New York where Manhattan parking can be forty-seven dollars per day. There are people who have lived here for many years who are just horrified about the growth. Like anywhere else, you have to accept growth and take the bad with the good. With growth comes rising incomes and a better life for the local people. We just have to accept that. Vallarta has one of the largest middle class populations in all of Mexico, and the boom is benefiting them with new cars and new homes. They're driving the growth of PV."

"I have great faith in the Mexican people," Len says. "Unfortunately, though, I think a lot of the people who move here come with the assumption that the Mexican people don't know anything. The Mexican people know a lot. They're playing catch-up, but things are improving."

CHAPTER NINE

CYNDEE RESTIVO

Married
Auburn, California
Semi-Retired

JOHN RESTIVO

Married
Auburn, California
Marshall, Vista Vallarta Golf Course

"We want one more adventure before we croak."

Cyndee and John Restivo have been baby boomer adventurers all their lives, restless and continually looking for new challenges that would enrich their relationship.

Born just after the Second World War ended in 1947, John grew up in San Francisco, where he graduated from high school. The family lived in the colorful North Beach section of the city when he was small, but they moved to the Westlake neighborhood of San Francisco in the mid-1950s when his butcher father and stay-at-home mom wanted more space for their five kids. John attended the City College of San Francisco for a few years and while there started working first in the retail grocery business and then the food service industry, which became his profession for seventeen years. At the same time, John worked for a high-profile amateur golfer at the San Francisco Golf Club, stirring his life-long passion for golf.

Fifty-eight-year-old Cyndee grew up in Sacramento in a home with a housewife mom and a dad who worked for the California Department of Water Resources. She lived there through her early twenties, receiving her BS in social work from California State University, Sacramento. Cindee was a true baby boomer adventurer like John, though, and heard the call to enlist in the Peace Corps. She served in West Africa for two years and then returned to her alma mater to receive her master's degree in social work in 1974.

The couple met in Sacramento on a blind date when John was working in the food service industry and Cyndee was in graduate school. It was love at first sight, a love that has lasted thirty-four years. They married and moved to a five-acre property in Auburn, California, a small town northeast of Sacramento in the Sierra Madre foothills, where John started a furniture restoration business in his barn and ran it for seven years. During that time he played "Mr. Mom" when Cyndee returned to work after having their first daughter.

Cyndee commuted to her job as a probation officer in Sacramento for ten years. "I hated that commute because it was an hour each way and kept getting worse," Cyndee remembers. "Our solution was to buy a gift store in Auburn, which I ran. We didn't know a thing about running a gift store, but we ran it successfully for seventeen years." John was on the road selling gifts, but he didn't find that job to his liking. Back home again, John started working for a friend in the hardwood flooring business, but the partnership was dissolved after a few years.

When the partnership ended, Cyndee suggested a real adventure: moving to Puerto Vallarta. "We had been coming to PV on vacation for twelve years, since 1992," she says. "The first time we were here we absolutely fell in love with the town. I had not been to Mexico before, and John's only travel experience had been in Guaymas. We always felt really at home in Vallarta and never had a desire to try any other place in Mexico."

"The idea of living in Mexico really started to click after we read a book called *On Mexican Time* that got us thinking about the possibilities," Cyndee recalls. "One night we were sitting out on the balcony at the time-share we had purchased at Playa del Sol, right on the beach at Playa de los Muertos. I asked John: 'Could you ever live down here?' He wasn't sure at the time because it wasn't in our realm of possibilities."

However, with the high cost of living in the States and not much of a retirement program, Puerto Vallarta began sounding more and more appealing to the couple. "Our family was not surprised at all when we decided to move to Puerto Vallarta because they had been with us on vacation and knew how wonderful it is and how much we loved it," Cyndee explains. "I had been working on a budget and thought if we stuck to our budget we could come down here earlier than we thought." Convinced that they could now afford the move, they started to research homes for sale in PV.

John and Cyndee started their house search on the Internet— as most do now—to see what they could afford. The couple knew that whatever they bought would probably have to be remodeled in some way, so they allocated funds for that. One thing was certain: they didn't want to live in a condo. "Coming from five acres of land in the Sierra foothills, we wanted a house," John says. "Once that decision was made, it was just a matter of finding the right house. We also spent quite a lot of time researching visa requirements and anything else that needed to be done before we actually moved here."

John was in Hawaii playing golf when Cyndee flew down to Puerto Vallarta to look at houses. She was fortunate that the sister of a good friend lived in PV, knew the city well, and was willing to help her look for a new home. "We went all over town looking at neighborhoods," Cyndee says. "I found that different people will give you different advice, but not all of it is accurate. Initially, we ran into several rather disreputable real estate agents. Luckily, we had a friend who was a lawyer who checked everything out for us."

Back in California, they began emptying a barn packed with furniture and memorabilia accumulated over twenty-seven years of marriage. "We had antique dealers coming for days," Cyndee remembers. They also had to go to the Mexican consulate in Sacramento to complete their list of furniture and other household and personal items they would be bringing with them to Mexico, called a *Menaje de Casa*. "It was very detailed," Cyndee says. "Even if you use a towel to wrap something in a box, the towel has to be included in the list and written on the packing box. They called us and said, 'Your list is in English but needs to be in Spanish.' I called my attorney friend in PV, and she was nice enough to do the whole list for us in Spanish. To this day, she still remembers what was in our boxes."

When they began shopping for a house, the couple wasn't looking for specific characteristics of a neighborhood, but rather value. They bought a three thousand square foot home with a pool just a block from the beach in the northern hotel zone, not far from the Krystal hotel, for under three hundred thousand dollars. "When our house sold in Auburn, we knew we had to make a final decision," Cyndee recalls. "Our real estate person really had not much to offer, so I found about four or five places to zero in on. When John walked into this house, he said, 'This is what I want.' John didn't want to live in many of the neighborhoods because of the noise: dogs, roosters, buses, cars, and often, loud music. If you buy a place in town, it's best to stay there for a few nights or just visit the property at night to see what it is really like."

"We love our home location because it really isn't a traditional neighborhood," Cyndee says. "We don't get the steady stream of knife salesmen at our door, the bread guy, or the plant guy. We are tucked away in a place that nobody knows about, and we like that just fine. Actually, our home and the two other houses next door were originally built for executives who ran the hotel Posada Vallarta, which is now the Krystal."

As a lifetime avid golfer, John would not have moved to PV if work at a local golf course had not been available. He worked at the Auburn, California, golf course for six years and has had a passion for the sport his entire life. "When we were planning on moving here, I talked with the general manager of the corporation that previously owned the world-class course, Vista Vallarta," John says. "He told me that I should be able to get a job at the course. After a bit of trying, I finally had a chance to meet with the person who now runs the golf operations at the course during one of my trips to PV. He said to come see him when I actually made the move. I stayed in touch, but when we finally moved here I was told that he couldn't hire me at that time. He did, however, recommend a job at the Mayan Palace golf course in Nuevo Vallarta. So, I went to see the head pro at that course, but he did not want to hire an expat. I then went back to Vista Vallarta, where things had changed since I last talked with them, and I finally was hired. I was so happy because I'm the kind of person who needs to stay busy. Of course, one of the great benefits is that both of us get to play golf at one of the best golf courses in the world in one of the most beautiful places in the world. And, we get to know so many people through working and golfing at Vista Vallarta."

Besides golf, Cyndee and John like people and food, in that order. They've found that the Mexican people are extremely warm and friendly and want to engage with you, even if you aren't fluent in Spanish. Cyndee speaks Spanish fairly well and reads local Spanish language newspapers. John says he speaks Spanish reasonably well, also. They had a private tutor for a while, spending an hour a day learning Spanish. As their lives became busier, though, they dropped the language lessons and are learning through immersion. "We have a number of Mexican friends who speak no English, and we get along fine with them," John says. During the summer John fires up the barbeque, and their Mexican friends come over to use the pool. "We have them decide what the menu should be, and then we buy the food and cook it."

They have had an easy time making Mexican friends in Vallarta. "It's fairly easy to meet Mexicans in PV," John concludes. "For example, the man who cuts my hair has a brother who opened a new restaurant. We went to the restaurant and became great friends with them and their family. They, in turn, introduced us to other people. Often we prefer to be with our Mexican friends than a lot of the expats we have met, mainly because many expats just aren't as genuine. Also, people have a tendency to reinvent themselves when they move here. And, as we have discovered, many of them probably should not even be here. In fact, some were upset that a lot of the television received here is not in English, and a few more were perplexed that the phone book is in Spanish. Some of the expats transplant their lifestyle from the United States or Canada and never quite integrate themselves into the community, that is, actually experience Mexico."

"People would ask us why we wanted to move to Puerto Vallarta, and we would say: 'We want one more adventure before we croak,'" Cyndee laughs. "And, we wanted that adventure to be meaningful. Interestingly, many Californians have no idea about Mexico or Mexicans. Their perception is migrant workers and the family that owns the local Mexican restaurant. We wanted our time here to be meaningful, and that means getting to know the people personally and integrating our lives into theirs. We know everyone in the area in which we live. If the dogs somehow get out, someone sees them and knows where to bring them back. They really look out for us. We're really in love with the Mexican people."

Food also is a passion for the couple. John—with his extensive experience in the food industry—appreciates the high-quality food available every day in PV. "Most of the fruits and vegetables never end up in cold storage but are sold fresh each day," John notes. "The quality, flavor, and freshness are outstanding, even though they may not last quite as long as the fruits and vegetables found up north. Beef is good here, also, and the fresh seafood is outstanding. We shop for food almost every day, the way many local people do. Soriana, our supermarket, is a block away, so it is easy to pop over and pick things up. The only drawback is when the bakery is going early in the morning and you can smell the fresh doughnuts, very dangerous. We both love Mexican pastries."

John and Cyndee also love the local restaurant scene but approach it differently now from when they first moved to PV. "When we first moved here, we tried many of the better restaurants in town but found that they are often as expensive as the restaurants in California," Cyndee remarks. "This is an international resort city, and we are on a fixed income, so we have to budget wisely. We did lots of exploring and now have a wide range of restaurants we go to in the local neighborhoods, where mainly Mexican workers live. We've found some marvelous places that are very inexpensive but have great ambience and food. There is a terrific restaurant also right across from the Vista Vallarta golf course that we go to frequently. The lady who owns it had a dinner for all of her regular customers and cooked a whole pig for us. It was beyond delicious."

Outside of golf, people, and food, Cyndee and John are not that involved with the local social whirl. "We have gotten involved in a small charity called New Life Mexico," Cyndee says. "I taught English for a year at their boys' center. It's a great feeling to help when we can. We don't, however, use charity work as a social event and a way to meet people. We have a small circle of expat friends, and that is plenty, considering how busy we usually are."

In addition to John's work at the golf course, Cyndee holds a part-time position at a local real estate firm to fill in a few more hours and pick up a few additional pesos, but for the most part they just like spending time at home together. "We're homebodies and not social at all," John admits. "We like each other's company, so the transition to Mexico has not been difficult. We've also developed some new interests to keep us entertained and busy. For example, we never used to be game players, but now we play cards and board games all of the time. And, Cyndee has started painting." "I started painting classes on a dare," adds Cyndee, "and it was the best thing I ever did. Now, I'm letting that creative child come back out."

The two are on a budget, so managing their expenses is a real concern. "The cost of living here is higher than we expected, but it's still less than living in California," Cyndee believes. "We paid seven thousand dollars a year in property tax for our house on five acres in Auburn, which was built in 1975. Here, we pay less than a thousand dollars for both our bank trust fee and property tax. Water seems to be very affordable, but electricity is not. We find it to be very expensive, but we have learned to conserve here."

Both agree that services are still fairly inexpensive, but where they think real money can be saved is the purchase of fruits, vegetables, and meat. "They're a lot cheaper than California," Cyndee notes. "You do have to stay away from the imported stuff, though. If you are looking for favorite American brands, be prepared to pay a lot. John knows his groceries—he started in the business pushing carts when he was just a kid—so I trust his judgment when it comes to food. We buy a lot of Mexican products and store brands and buy a lot of fruits off the local trucks."

They also believe that housing is still a good value in Puerto Vallarta in spite of the big run-up in prices over the last few years. "There is a wide range of properties available for most pocketbooks, but one thing to look out for," John cautions, "is condo fees, especially if a number of units are time-share. They run their electricity all day long, and if each unit doesn't have a separate meter, watch out. The best deals we found are in the local neighborhoods. If you are willing to live in a mostly Mexican neighborhood, you can get some excellent values. We say take a chance. Learn the language and the culture to help you fit in. If you need help to assimilate, we recommend the book *There's a Word for It in Mexico* that we use all of the time. It is very good for explaining cultural differences."

Both agree that things have changed in PV since they moved here in 2005. "There is a lot more traffic, high-rise condos are going up along the bay, parking is even harder to find, and there may be a bit more crime," John says. "Crime really isn't a problem here, but we did have a small credit card problem a while back. We got a phone call one day from a man in Texas who wanted to know if we were ready to take delivery of our fighting cocks! You do have to be careful using both credit and ATM cards here."

John thinks that growth does bring some real benefits, though. "Cyndee and I do like the new Liverpool department store in the Galleria and the new Soriana supermarket that's just a couple of blocks from our house. When we speak with the taxi drivers or our Mexican friends, they're the first ones to say that the growth is creating more jobs for people and improving local economic conditions. Who are we to complain about the very things that are improving their lives and life-styles?"

Their biggest wish, however, is that Vallarta does not become Acapulco in ten years. The local newspapers often call the development that is happening in Puerto Vallarta the "Acapulcoization" of Vallarta. It is a pejorative that reflects the negative consequences of the uncontrolled growth that city experienced. "Even if it does, we probably wouldn't move to an outlying area because as you get older, you have to be mindful of your health and accessibility to health care facilities," John says. "But, most importantly, we couldn't live without close access to golf and all of the other things we have come to love about Vallarta."

Chapter Ten

Jim Keil

Committed Partner
Nevada City, California
Retired

Pamela Olson

Committed Partner
Nevada City, California
Retired

"Maybe now is the time to look for that place on the
beach that used to be Puerto Vallarta."

The path to their tropical paradise can be a circuitous route
for many baby boomers, but it ran directly through the Internet
for Northern California boomers Jim Keil and Pamela Olson.
In 2000, the couple connected online, and after five months
of telephone conversations, they met, fell in love, and started
dreaming about living their lives in Puerto Vallarta.

Just shy of sixty-two, Jim grew up in Sacramento, California, and graduated from California State University, Sacramento, with a business degree. Jim's father was in accounting

before he decided to switch careers and join a car dealership, which he eventually purchased and owned for over fifty years. The switch pleased Jim's mom and two siblings but made Jim even happier.

He started working in his father's automobile business when he was in high school, sweeping floors, running parts, and washing cars. Shortly before graduation from college, he got a promotion to the dealership's office. Now on a management track, Jim soon moved over to the leasing division of the company and eventually ran that business for over ten years.

In 1982, Jim tired of the car business and tried his hand in construction for a while but quickly realized that his heart was still in the car business. He began searching for a dealership to run, and in 1984 he found it in Grass Valley, California, located about forty miles north of Sacramento. Jim Keil Chevrolet opened its doors twenty-four years ago. "Grass Valley is a small town of about twelve thousand people," Jim details, "but the surrounding area population is around seventy-five thousand. It has a very rich history as one of the leading gold producing areas in California." Jim lived in Grass Valley's sister city, Nevada City, a town with a population of thirty-five hundred.

Fifty-four year old Pamela Olson was born in Yreka, California, far north, close to the Oregon border. Her dad logged for a living while her schoolteacher mom taught and raised Pamela, her brother, and two sisters. Later, the family moved to Redding, California, where Pamela graduated from high school and then went on first to the College of the Redwoods in Eureka, on California's northern coast, and then to San Diego State. While in school, Pamela went to Europe and, like many other baby boomers, decided not to return to college. She moved back to Redding, got married, and started a family, but that was not to last. Divorce entered her life, so she started a bookkeeping business specializing primarily in helping contractors in Redding, which she did for most of her life.

Her life changed quickly at the turn of the century, though, when she met Jim online, moved to Nevada City to be with him in 2001, and got her real estate license and a job with a local firm.

Jim and Pamela were regular visitors to Puerto Vallarta before they met. Pamela started vacationing in PV in 1980 when she was still married and then came regularly after her divorce in the late 1980s, traveling alone and usually staying at the Sheraton, a place that became both familiar and comfortable for her. After vacationing in Zihuatanejo, Cozumel, and Cabo, she fell in love with PV's people and the beauty of its natural setting.

Jim also had been a frequent visitor to Vallarta since the '80s. His parents owned a time-share at Costa Vida on the south shore—now called Playa del Sol Costa Sur—and invited him to vacation with them in 1985. He liked it so much that when his one-week stay was over, he was the proud owner of four weeks of time-share at the place. That started Jim's annual trips to PV. Other than a jaunt to Tijuana, Jim never ventured to any other city in Mexico.

After Jim and Pamela joined their lives in 2001, they began vacationing at Jim's time-share two or three times a year, soon increasing his time-share amount to seven weeks. While visiting in 2005, friends they had met at Costa Vida decided to look for a place to own instead of using their time-share. Their friends found a condo in the area south of the Cuale River, which got Pamela and Jim interested in looking for their own place.

"After seeing their new condo, we got excited and started thinking about the possibilities of owning a home in PV," Jim remembers. "When we got home, we talked about it and then called the realtor that sold the condo to our friends and told them we would like to purchase a unit there, also. We flew back five weeks later to buy it but, after looking at it again, decided it wasn't exactly what we wanted to buy. That's when we started looking for a house to rent for the following winter. We thought it would be better to live here for a while to help us decide if we really wanted to live in Vallarta full time. The last place we looked at was a house in Mismaloya that was both for rent and sale. We liked the location, just seven miles south of Puerto Vallarta on a hill overlooking Mismaloya cove, so we decided to buy the house, rather than rent."

Now, with a house of their own, Jim and Pamela began visiting two weeks every other month and found they loved living in paradise. In October of 2005, they packed up their furniture and headed south of the border for what they thought at the time would be a six-month stay, the traditional "snow bird" high season living in PV. But after just a few months, the couple knew they wanted to live in Vallarta year-round. Deciding to live full-time, though, opened up a new discussion between the two.

Pamela was all for living full time but wanted a larger house, particularly a property with a lawn large enough for their two standard poodles. The house in Mismaloya was thirty-five hundred square feet with three bedrooms, three and a half baths, and a beautiful view of the bay, but the land was limited and occupied primarily by a large pool and deck on the ocean side and parking on the jungle side.

In the spring of 2006, after several months of new home shopping, the couple zeroed in on a fifty-five hundred square foot home on a third of an acre of land in the prestigious hillside development of Sierra del Mar, just above the Presidente Inter-continental hotel on the south coast. Jim and Pamela loved the space for the dogs and the area's microclimate, which receives more rain and is cooler than the city.

Now settled in to their piece of paradise, Pamela and Jim took their first step into the local culture by enrolling in a three-week Spanish class. "The class was very good with lots of homework but a big time commitment," says Pamela. Although they practice Spanish every day with their employees and Mexican friends, their Spanish is still not fluent. However, Pamela doesn't believe that being fluent in Spanish is absolutely necessary, given the prevalence of a large English-speaking local community that supports the tourism industry. She acknowledges, though, that knowing Spanish shows respect and is just a practical thing to do, particularly for traveling within Mexico.

The pursuit of the perfect retirement lifestyle for Jim and Pamela includes working out at their favorite gym on the south side of town every day for a couple of hours, reading, and golf. "We don't belong to any of the local expat organizations or charities, but we support them," Pamela admits. She also attends the monthly expat "breakfast club" held at various restaurants around town to meet new people. Jim dedicates part of his time to serving as treasurer for the Sierra del Mar homeowners' association.

Jim is also involved as an investor in a major new real estate development on the Costa Allegre. In April 2006, his real estate agent and attorney invited him to take a look at some coastal land about two hours' drive south of Vallarta. The closest village to the property is called José Maria Morales. "I ended up making a land purchase in the area known as Playa Chalacatepic," Jim informs. "The primary motivation to purchase property located so far from Vallarta was the knowledge that a new international airport was going to be built in the area by the state of Jalisco. The airport had not been started at the time

I purchased the property, but it was estimated that they would start building the airport within a year and a half to two years. It is now finally underway. The setting is marvelous, a combination of beachfront, meadows, and a freshwater lake. Every spot on the property has an ocean view. Eventually the property will be developed, probably with a joint venture partner."

Living in a privileged area, the expat couple doesn't often bump up against many of the negative sides of living in Puerto Vallarta, except when vehicles are involved. "I get very nervous about driving downtown, especially with the narrow streets and so many buses, and they are all driving too fast and competing with each other for passengers," Pamela laments. Jim agrees with Pamela on the buses and adds that aggressive taxi drivers who often ignore traffic regulations can also be a hazard. "Mexicans are very laid-back and easygoing people, but an interesting change occurs when they get behind the wheel of an automobile," Jim says. "They become the craziest people in the world. Driving can be very dangerous here. I see both buses and cars passing on blind curves all of the time. You have to be what I call aggressively defensive in your driving down here to stay out of trouble."

Jim notes that the driving experience also includes having to put up with minor aggravations from the transit police. "They seem to like to pull over cars with American license plates. I've been stopped a half a dozen times in the last three years, primarily, I think, because both of our vehicles carry California plates. We had one interesting experience driving home from town that was a bit frustrating. Our vehicle was last in a row of about six cars headed south on the coastal highway when a police officer pulled us over and told us we were driving too fast. I said that I was the last vehicle in a line of six cars and if I was speeding, everyone was. He didn't seem to care about that and said we were exceeding the forty kilometers per hour speed limit. I reminded him that the speed limit was actually sixty kilometers per hour once you left the city. He then switched gears and said that I had gone around the curve too fast. Next, he asked to see all of our documents. Finally, he asked where we lived, and we told him just a few miles down the road. By now he was quite frustrated, got in his car, and sped off without giving us any ticket. We caught up with him again about another mile down the road and watched him pull over another car from the middle of a line of cars, this time a Jeep full of tourists. I guess he was working on his quota that day."

Pamela and Jim agree, though, that for every "bad cop" story there is an uplifting one about random acts of good will in Vallarta. Not long ago, they were in a taxi and Pamela inadvertently left her wallet in the back seat. "I never thought I would see it again," Pamela says. "After I discovered that I had left it in the taxi, we went back to the taxi stand by Rizzo's on the south side to look for the taxi we had taken, but it wasn't there. We then called the taxi dispatcher's office to report my missing wallet. I didn't know the taxi number or any other information. At that time, my left wrist was in a cast, so the taxi drivers recognized me. A supervisor at the taxi stand took us on an hour trek around town searching for the driver of the cab and also took us to the dispatcher's house. After going full circle and arriving back at the taxi stand, the taxi we had used drove up, and the driver presented me with my wallet with all the contents intact. How often does that happen north of the border?" Pamela also recounts another act of goodwill: "We met friends for dinner downtown one evening, and they told us they had left a bottle of tequila in their taxi. Before we had finished dinner, the taxi driver returned to the restaurant, found the couple, and returned their bottle of tequila."

The rapid growth of Vallarta in the past several years, however, has put a strain on the city and its well-known friendliness. Pamela and Jim now have begun thinking about moving to a smaller town more like Puerto Vallarta used to be when they first began visiting here, either north or south of the city. "Being on the beach in a small town would be ideal," Jim muses. "In the next ten years, probably all of the available land around the bay will be developed. Maybe now is the time to look for that place on the beach that used to be Puerto Vallarta."

CHAPTER ELEVEN

CYNTHIA SAMS

Married
Ottawa, Canada
Agent, Coldwell Banker La Costa Real Estate

ANDRE RIVIÉRE

Married
Ottawa, Canada
Agent, LandBankers International/Sierra Madre
Holdings

"You know it's all about expectations when you move here, but the reality you find is a less than perfect paradise."

Cynthia Sams and Andre Riviére are Canadian baby boomers who were smitten by the beauty and romance of Puerto Vallarta, but they soon learned that perception is not always reality.

Andre, fifty-two, was born and raised in Cornwall, Ontario, a small paper mill town in eastern Canada, but moved to Ottawa to attend college at Algonquin, where he majored in youth and family counseling. He worked in that field for twenty years with both private and local and state government institutions. But after twenty years in his field of study, he felt he needed a change, so he returned to school to get his real estate license and started working for Century 21 in the Ottawa area, where he worked as a realtor for nine years.

Cynthia was born on Quebec's Gaspe Peninsula fifty years ago but headed for Ottawa as soon as she turned seventeen to attend Carleton University, where she received her degree in sociology and political science. She worked in social work for a few years and then went on to the University of Ottawa for her law degree. Her first job out of law school was corporate counsel for a very large union. However, Cynthia was an entrepreneur at heart and soon started her own law firm, which flourished for many years. Immediately prior to moving to Vallarta, she was part of a legal association with several other lawyers.

Andre and Cynthia have been married for over twenty years and during that time often vacationed in Mexico with their children, a son and a daughter. Their travels took them to Cancun, Mazatlan, and Guadalajara, but they didn't make it to Puerto Vallarta until the Christmas holiday of 2003. The couple had been discussing the idea of moving to a foreign country for at least six years prior to their Vallarta vacation because they were intrigued with the idea of exposing their children to a different culture and language, at least for a period of time.

The main thing holding Cynthia and Andre back from implementing their plan to live in another country was their concern about how the children would adapt. Those concerns, however, were swept away during that Christmas of 2003. Their parents were no longer living, Cynthia was an only child, and Andre's only brother had passed away, so they felt they had no strong ties to hold them in Canada any longer. Both had done a lot of traveling when they were younger and were driven by a strong sense of adventure.

Adventure called to the two baby boomers one evening as they strolled along a beach in Vallarta that Christmas. "I have always been an adventurous person," Cynthia explains. "I was looking at our life and really wanted a change, to see more of the world." Her father had recently passed away, which in some sense freed her to explore living their dream. "The sun was going down over the bay, and we had just had a marvelous three-week vacation in Mexico. We just looked at each other and said, 'We can live here.'"

"We met several couples on our Christmas trip in 2003 who lived in Vallarta full-time and worked in the time-share business," Andre recalls. "They encouraged us to move to Vallarta. It was a real eye opener for us because, until we met our new friends, we thought the only Americans and Canadians who lived down here were retired."

The big question they faced was how they were going to support themselves and their two children with no retirement income. They flew home to think things through and stayed in contact with their new friends via e-mail and telephone. Cynthia was becoming burned-out on law and looking for a new adventure, and they had no family to hold them in Canada, so the couple was in a perfect situation to act on their dream. They had sold their large home on a lake in the hills north of Ottawa and were renting a place at that time to decide what to do next.

Their decision to move to Vallarta was made easier six weeks after they returned home when Andre was offered a job selling time-share at the Mayan Palace in Nuevo Vallarta. Andre was elated. "What's the worst case scenario? We go down, we bomb out, and after a year we come back to Canada and continue our lives." They kept a property they owned on the

Gaspe Peninsula that was fully furnished, to ensure a fall back position in case things didn't work out in PV.

When they returned to Vallarta in February of 2004, Andre started working at the Mayan Palace, and Cynthia began looking for a rental home for the family and a school for the children. "When I flew home and left Andre behind, it was one of the hardest days of my life," Cynthia remembers. "We had never been apart in all of our years of marriage. Plus, it was one of the coldest winters Canada had seen in years. I looked at our two children and wondered what we had done."

Cynthia was still working but now added the responsibility of getting everything organized for the move. She bought several how-to books on moving to Mexico but felt they over-complicated things. "The books didn't provide either accurate or practical advice," she complains. "A lot of what they tell you with regards to required paperwork, for example, was not necessary." As a classic Type-A personality, Cynthia was well suited to organize the move. "I had an additional incentive. I was throwing logs on the fire every few minutes it seemed, and Andre was sitting around the pool drinking margaritas. That made me really committed to making the move," Cynthia chuckles.

To begin the moving process, she began selling off antiques, artwork, and other non-essential items they had accumulated over twenty years of marriage. The remaining furniture was moved to their house on the Gaspe Peninsula. "People need to be told to get rid of most of their things," Cynthia says. "You just don't need all that stuff down here. It also costs a lot of money to ship things to Mexico, so be very, very careful about what you bring, especially furniture that is not hardwood or treated for termites."

Andre, still enthusiastic about selling time-share and living in PV, flew back to Canada in May to help with the move.

Cynthia had gotten everything ready, so they loaded up their SUV and trailer with their personal things and headed south. Crossing the border was uneventful, and the drive down was not stressful. The family moved into a furnished rented house in the Marina area. "Finding good, well-priced rental homes in Vallarta can sometimes be difficult because property owners can make more from short-term vacation rentals," Cynthia notes. "We took a one-year lease with an eye to moving back to Canada after a year if things didn't work out the way we wanted."

Now settled, Cynthia enrolled the children in the nearby American School in the Marina, an elite, bilingual school for the children of expats and wealthy Mexicans. They chose the school after researching several options because the school communicated well with them, had high academic standards, and good extra curricular activities. In addition, the school had just over three hundred students in K–12, so they knew their children would receive lots of personal attention. "A plus for putting our kids in the American School was that they awarded American accreditation upon graduation, which we knew was very important for college-level placement," Cynthia says. "The downside is the tuition, enrollment fees, and expenses, which run nearly ten thousand dollars per year, per student."

Even with the high cost, the couple is pleased with the school. "It has a pretty good sports program, and the music program is also good," Cynthia remarks. "It's probably the highest quality education available in Puerto Vallarta. Most of the teachers have master's degrees and are mainly from the United States and Canada. Andre and I think the school here is actually better than the public schools in Canada. And, very importantly, our son told us that he saw fewer drugs in high school in PV than the elementary grades in Canada." The school initially was a challenge for their daughter because she had been in a French-speaking school in Canada but now had to use both English and Spanish daily.

After several years with the school, the couple continues to be very happy with their choice and has gotten to know a few of the families of the children who attend the school. Friendships are important to Andre and Cynthia. They were looking forward to developing relationships with many Mexicans when they moved to PV, but that has not happened. Cynthia readily admits that not being fluent in Spanish is probably the main barrier to developing a wide circle of Mexican friends. They have, however, developed many friendships with like-minded expats. "We find our PV friends very interesting, real adventurers, and risk takers," Cynthia says. "They have interesting lives, are easygoing, more open, and often less judgmental than many of our friends back home in Canada."

Andre exited the time-share business and moved on to a large real estate development group—LandBankers International/Sierra Madre Holdings—a company that is developing land near the new international airport construction south of Puerto Vallarta on the Costa Allegre. "The company buys land in the path of growth and then installs the infrastructure necessary to increase the value of the land," Andre explains. "It has land in several countries, but their main focus at the moment is south of PV, which is the real future for this area."

The development is located fifty miles south of Puerto Vallarta and has over five miles of beachfront spread over ten thousand acres of land, about the size of PV. Only six miles from the new airport and seven miles from the town of Tomatlan, the development is called Brisas del Pacifico. The beauty of the area is very compelling to Andre and Cynthia. "The beaches in this emerging new resort area are far superior to the Bay of Banderas beaches," Andre says. "In ten years or less when the area is more developed and the children are out of school, we'll probably move to this new area."

Cynthia also needed to work, and time-share beckoned. She spent about a year and a half toiling in time-share before she decided that it was not for her. She then parlayed her newly discovered sales abilities first into a job with a resort developer, helping to set up the sales office for the development, and then as the sales manager for a small resort for a year. When it was sold, though, she was without work again and decided to take some time off.

After running her own legal firm in Canada, Cynthia had a difficult time accepting the jobs she found available in PV for English-speaking expats. She was almost ready to throw in the towel when she read an article in a local English language newspaper about a new manager who had just started working at the local Coldwell Banker real estate office. Knowing the owner of the firm through the American School, she decided to apply for a real estate job at Coldwell Banker, got it, and has been working for them for a year. "The options for work down here are fairly limited," Cynthia says. "Basically, you have time-share, real estate, or you can start your own business. That's about it."

Now that they are part of Vallarta's expat community and living their dream in Mexico, Cynthia and Andre are using the time to enrich the lives of their children, as well as themselves. They recently visited the Mexican state of Michoacan to see the winter migration area for monarch butterflies and are planning a trip to visit the Copper Canyon of northern Mexico. They also keep their children culturally reconnected through what they call "reverse" vacations, like skiing in the Colorado Rockies and driving down the coast of California.

Besides the over three hundred days of sunshine each year that help enable Vallarta's vaunted weather, Cynthia and Andre also love Vallarta's free and easy lifestyle but still get frustrated now and then when they bump up against the local "system." When Cynthia first got her driver's license, she paid a bribe or *mordida*—as it is colorfully known—to help pave the way and make the process easier and faster. However, when her wallet was stolen and she had to replace her license, she decided to follow the Mexican system. After three trips to renew her license and many frustrations, she gave up and brought in a colleague from work who knew all the right people and could get her license renewed with no hassle, but a little extra money. She and Andre have concluded—as many expats living in PV have—that developing a network of local people who know how to get things done and paying a bribe when necessary is often a wise move to help limit the level of frustration in dealing with the "system."

"If you come down here to retire, it's much less frustrating," says Cynthia. "You can insulate yourself from so many of the day-to-day frustrations we experience. But if you have children and are working here, the reality is that you have to deal with a lot of bureaucracy, and often it is corrupt, unreasonable, illogical, time-consuming, and just plain difficult to deal with." They have given their children identification cards with their attorney's name and number on them to use if they run into any problems. "You just can't count on the local authorities to do the right thing," Cynthia laments, "so the cards—and cell phones—are essential for the children to carry."

The romantic moonlight walk on the beach four years ago now seems a long time ago. The reality of everyday living in Vallarta has taken a bit of the romance out of living here for the couple. "You know it's all about expectations when you move here, but the reality you find is a less-than-perfect paradise," Cynthia concludes.

CHAPTER TWELVE

JOHN YOUDEN

Married
Prince Rupert, British Columbia
Publisher/Editor-in-Chief,
Vallarta Lifestyles Group

"Back then everyone congregated at one or two places,
and it was easy to make friends and stay in touch with
everyone."

John Youden is a fifty-year-old baby boomer entrepreneur
from Canada's west coast who built a Puerto Vallarta publishing empire in less than twenty years. His publications include
Vallarta Lifestyles, *Costa Vallarta*, *Vallarta Real Estate Guide*,
Vallarta Nautica, and a number of popular Web sites, including
a site for Mexico Boutique Hotels. He is widely recognized as
a leading authority on Puerto Vallarta and the more expansive
Costa Vallarta.

John has flourished in paradise, building a multi-faceted
publishing business from Vallarta's first multi-listing service
for the real estate industry in the late 1980s. After running the
MLS service for a year, local realtors asked John if he would develop a color publication to help promote the Bay of Banderas
area. Desktop publishing had just taken off at that time, so he

published the very early version of what was to become *Vallarta Lifestyles* magazine, a spectacularly successful glossy publication that has grown to over three hundred pages today.

John's next publication was called *Yachts and Villas*, which he launched in 1992 and continued until 1999. He sold the boating, travel, and real estate magazine in 1999. *Costa Vallarta* was launched seven years ago and focuses on upscale home furnishings. John is quick to point out that the name encompasses the entire region from the Riviera Nayarit to the north and the Costa Allegre to the south, not just Puerto Vallarta. *Vallarta Real Estate Guide* is a free monthly publication that John started at the same time as *Costa Vallarta*. His publishing firm also produces several glossy coffee-table books about Vallarta that are marketed through local newsstands and bookstores.

John's businesses also include online properties that have grown out of his interests. When John travels within Mexico promoting his publications, he likes to stay at small boutique hotels. "I kept hearing from all of the hotels that they had a difficult time marketing their properties. So I thought if all of them could work together on their marketing and share a standard of quality, we could create a marketable brand they could use. That idea has been transformed into our Mexico Boutique Hotels business, which includes forty-five small, upscale hotels throughout Mexico that we market both online and off-line. We operate it as a separate business from our publishing group. It is now a recognizable brand of quality that many travelers and travel agents rely on."

John arrived in PV in 1988 to get away from the cold Canadian winter for a month. He had been to Mexico on vacation before but not to Puerto Vallarta. He liked what he saw, bought a time-share, and then came back three times that year to use it. "I was in real estate in Canada but getting a little tired of it," John recollects. "I decided to take a year or two

off and go back to Mexico and work in the time-share industry, which I did for the first year I was here in 1989. During
that time, I met a guy who wanted to start a publication and
had just bought all of the publishing equipment, but he didn't
know how to build a database. I had just developed a database
in northern Canada and knew what needed to be done. I wrote
the program for him so he could get his business going. In less
than a year, he grew tired of the business, and I bought him
out and took the business over. He had given me half of it for
developing the program, anyway. So, that ended the idea of
leaving Vallarta after a year or two."

John didn't speak Spanish when he first arrived in PV. "It
was either sink or swim, and I wanted to eat," says the now fluent John. He was from a small town of twelve thousand people
in northern British Columbia called Prince Rupert, located
just below the Alaska Panhandle. "What I loved about this
town when I first arrived was the weather, especially important for someone who came from northern Canada where the
weather was even worse than Seattle's. The idea that you could
go into the water at any time and find it warm was a novel
idea. Vallarta was also very different from most of the places I
had been. I had traveled to Europe and liked it and soon discovered that many of the same things I had enjoyed there also
existed in Puerto Vallarta. I liked the people very much and
found something deep inside me telling me that this is where
I really do belong. I loved the concept of living in the tropics.
It really wasn't until I started traveling around Mexico for my
publication *Yachts and Villas* that I realized how lucky I was in
choosing Puerto Vallarta as a place to live."

Puerto Vallarta was a small town when John first arrived,
which he enjoyed very much. "Back then everyone congregated
at one or two places, and it was easy to make friends and stay
in touch with everyone. It was harder, though, to earn a living

at that time with such a small population base. But as the area has expanded and my audience base has grown, my business has become far more profitable. For the past five or six years, Vallarta has just boomed. I attribute our startling growth rate to the baby boomers. The terrible tragedy in 2001, I think, was a wake-up call for all of America. Americans work very hard, but after that event I think they stepped back, reassessed their lives, and decided that they wanted more out of life. Not long after 9-11, we saw a large increase in families and couples coming to PV to look for a second home that they could enjoy for varying lengths of time. Boomers are also getting to that age when they begin looking for a place where they can escape winter."

John explains that Puerto Vallarta is still primarily a second-home market for both houses and condominiums, fueled in part by the large increases in home equity generated, particularly in the early- to mid-2000s in the U.S. and Canada. "This market is still primarily a cash market, but much of that cash comes from existing home equity. Financing wasn't available here until just the last several years and is still not widely used."

Although fondly remembering a smaller, less hectic Vallarta, John thinks that baby boomer-generated growth is here to stay and has adopted strategies to maintain his equilibrium. "My wife Florence and I prefer the small town that Vallarta once was, but on the business side, we like the large, growing city. We have adapted by adopting a dual life here. We have a family property in the Punta de Mita area on the north shore of the bay and for the past five or six years have been using it as a weekend place. When our two kids get out of school late Friday afternoon, we head north for a relaxing weekend and then return to PV on Sunday night. We call it our 'cabin at the lake,'" John laughs. But now that his kids are older, it is primarily John and Florence who use their Punta de Mita get-away, adding Wednesdays to split the workweek. "We do enjoy our time in Vallarta, though, because it has all the services we like. The only thing the city doesn't really offer, though, is a full spectrum of cultural events and offerings, but that's a good reason to go on vacation."

John points out that one of the side effects of the rapid growth in Vallarta is the tight labor market. "We pay above market rates for people and still have a difficult time finding employees. The competition here for people is aggressive. Almost anyone can find work in Puerto Vallarta. The low unemployment and rising incomes tied to the growth of the city is a big part of the traffic and parking issues we have here, which is actually a good thing. For example, our company has twenty-five employees. Six years ago only four or five of them would have had cars. Now, every person in the office has a car. It's the prosperity that growth has brought that has impacted the traffic, parking, and other problems we now face."

The growth of the local real estate market can only be described as a boom for the last five years. According to the sales data tabulated by John's publications, the average sales price of a home in the Puerto Vallarta area was $256,000 in 2003, but nearly tripled to $693,000 by 2007. For condos, the average 2003 price was $196,000, but leaped to $351,000 by 2007. Last year, seventeen hundred homes and condos were sold in the PV area.

"During the last several years, we have seen the start of major new home and condo development projects that were approved by the city administration that left office at the end of 2006," John states. "Most of the new developments are being built in the area north of Puerto Vallarta. The north has flatter, more construction-friendly land, which therefore is lower in price. What is amazing to me, though, is the number of properties now that are listed at one million dollars or more, compared with just several years ago. Four or five years ago we hardly sold million-dollar homes, but now it happens frequently. Luckily, there are still many projects being built that start in the two hundred fifty thousand dollar price range."

The growth Vallarta has been experiencing may or may not continue, according to John. He thinks at this time it is difficult to say whether or not the local market will be affected by the housing crisis in the U.S. "Anecdotally, the fact that many realtors have been hard to reach suggests that the market is still doing well," John surmises, "suggesting that they are too busy to return e-mails or phone calls."

John estimates that there could be as many as twenty thousand expats living in Vallarta, which would make it the second largest concentration of expatriates in Mexico, just behind the Lake Chapala area south of Guadalajara. He acknowledges that there are no hard numbers to substantiate that figure, but recent growth rates tend to support the number. "The majority are still second home snowbirds, those who stay during the November through April high season. Those that live in PV year-round usually own just one residence."

After twenty years of flourishing in PV, John has a few ideas on how boomers can get the most out of living in Vallarta. "The single best thing to improve the quality of life here is networking, especially for those people who come down for six months each year. The boomer moving into retirement now is very different from the retiree of twenty years ago. In that bygone era, retirees were comfortable having cocktails in the afternoon, relaxing at the beach, and then going out for something to eat. Then, they would do it all over again the next day. Retirees now are more proactive, probably have something still going on in the United States, and are still working, perhaps part-time, but not necessarily. They need things to do. Some have gotten into real estate, some are into art, many participate in nonprofit work, and a few start their own small businesses, usually retail stores. There has to be a way to plug into a network to find out what is going on in your area of interest. We are constantly working on ways we can help that social interaction take place. One idea is the development of a network that allows people who visit and those who live here to know what is available for supporting nonprofits, either financially or getting in there and helping out. The problem now is that nothing is in just one place. You have to go looking for the information in a lot of different places, which is inconvenient. Stay tuned for more developments in this area."

As a leading expat expert on the area, John holds strong views on what the future holds for Puerto Vallarta. "I think that in ten years, Puerto Vallarta will become a service center for this coastline. Those people who moved here for the small town ambience will be moving to the outlying areas of the north shore or the south shore. Puerto Vallarta will provide the services necessary for them. Also, and I think very importantly, Puerto Vallarta as a city will remain very viable because we have been able to retain the look and feel of the downtown area, which is so important to the Puerto Vallarta brand name. Cabo San Lucas doesn't have it. Mazatlan doesn't have it. Acapulco destroyed it. It's really what makes us unique. Vallarta also is ahead of the game for having any type of networks for what people can do with their time, better than anywhere else, except perhaps the Lake Chapala area. The problem with Chapala, however, is that everything shuts down early at night. It's more of the old-style retirement where no one works. I don't think that is where active baby boomers want to go. We have a whole different trend of active retirement and living that is taking place here in Vallarta, driven very much by baby boomers."

CHAPTER THIRTEEN

ALLYNA VINEBERG

Divorced
Montreal, Canada
Editor, *Vallarta Tribune*

"I hope fervently for an honest administration that will actually implement some of the excellent plans they have been developing over the years. The operative word here is implement."

The *Vallarta Tribune* weekly newspaper is the English voice of the expat community in Puerto Vallarta, treading a careful line between information tourists need to know and news expats want to know.

The paper and its Spanish language sister publication *Tribuna de la Bahia* are owned by Señor Fernando Gonzalez Corona, who is a former mayor of Puerto Vallarta, former federal deputy, and a wealthy businessman with assets in a number of Mexican states. The *Vallarta Tribune* is distributed through a wide range of physical locations throughout the bay. Eighty percent of the paper's distribution is through tourist hotels, galleries, and restaurants, while the other 20 percent goes to condos and central distribution points for local residents.

As the paper's editor, sixty-two-year-old Allyna Vineberg has to deal with the rising demand by expats who live in Puerto Vallarta for more news that focuses on their needs, rather than tourists. Because of the paper's editorial slant toward tourism and the advertising it brings in, she is somewhat restricted from publishing more controversial stories that affect Vallarta. The only sections of the paper that present a more unvarnished look at PV are the authentic opinions expressed in the "Letters from Readers" segment and the "She Said" column, written by Anna Reisman. "We are trying to be more relevant and topical through Anna's column, but we have to remember that she was nearly deported in August of 1999 because of some of the things she had written," Allyna explains. "But, Anna has her Mexican citizenship now and can be a lot bolder in presenting stories that need to be told, which I know will both please and inform our expat readers."

Boomer Allyna Vineberg joined the publication in 1997 after arriving in Vallarta from Montreal, Canada, three years earlier. That first year, Allyna and her partner opened Vallarta's first and only professional video production facility, producing all of the promotional videos for the big hotels and Puerto Vallarta's tourism bureau.

Allyna was married for twenty-five years while living in Montreal and raised a daughter and two sons. Prior to moving to PV, multilingual Allyna held a number of interesting jobs in Montreal over the years, including graphic artist, real estate administrator, and legal translator, but she was always looking for a spark that would change the direction of her life. She found it in the form of the famous motivational speaker Anthony Robbins. She and her partner attended a workshop that Robbins held in Montreal in the early 1990s, and soon everything changed for them. "That experience, coupled with one of the worst winters Montreal had experienced in years, put us on a plane heading south for a week in Puerto Vallarta's sunshine," Allyna remembers.

On the flight to Puerto Vallarta, Allyna's partner, who had worked for the Canadian Broadcasting Company (CBC) for twenty-six years, came up with the idea to start a video production company. Their week of relaxation turned out to be a whirlwind week of selling that idea to prospective buyers. And besides promoting their production idea, Allyna decided to purchase a house. "It was one of those Anthony Robbins things," she laughs. "Fifty-one percent of the whole thing is decision. I fell in love with this house and got so excited that I didn't sleep all night." The next morning she made an offer and soon became a PV homeowner.

Allyna had vacationed in Puerto Vallarta in 1992 and had fallen in love with everything about the tropical paradise. She decided then that when she retired PV would be her place of choice. In the preceding ten years, she had traveled to many other cities in Mexico, but she clearly left her heart in Vallarta. She loved the climate and the similarity between PV and Portofino, Italy, both towns with mountains cascading down to the sea.

As editor of the leading English language newspaper in Puerto Vallarta, Allyna realizes that she plays a significant role in shaping tourist and expat attitudes toward the city and Mexico in general. She tries to speak out on topics that are important to both audiences. "The rapid growth of Puerto Vallarta that we have seen in the last four or five years has put a real strain on the infrastructure of the city," she notes. "Traffic seems to be the number one complaint of locals and visitors. Driving here can sometimes be quite chaotic. You know, Mexico has some of the best laws in the world, but so many of them are not enforced, which can be very frustrating. Traffic laws are a primary example. Driving can be a real experience here because so few obey the laws, the biggest culprits being the buses and the taxis. The local transit police have introduced radar guns, breathalyzers, and other modern tools to help enforce the traffic laws, but you still have to be extremely defensive when you drive in Puerto Vallarta. Drivers are very aggressive and often don't follow the rules. One of the strange anomalies of local law, for example, can be found in the bizarre dichotomy of seat belt laws. The current law only applies to those within the vehicle. If you do not have your seat belt on, you can be liable for a ticket. However, if you are driving a truck and transporting people in the back of the truck, they do not have to wear a seat belt. And in Mexico, that can be as many as a dozen people or more."

She thinks city buses are also a big part of the traffic problem and is frustrated that the city seems to be powerless to deal with them. "With three bus companies and far too many bus routes in the downtown area, congestion has gotten much worse," Allyna complains. "Because there are so many, buses compete for customers, which in turn forces them to race each other to the next stop to pick up as many riders as they can. Fatalities caused by buses hitting pedestrians are a problem here. The families of pedestrians struck and killed by buses by law receive only six thousand dollars in compensation. When a bus driver runs over someone, he runs for the hills. A lawyer friend of mine told me when I first moved here that if you're ever in an accident, make sure you run over them until they're dead. That way you only have to pay the six thousand dollars. Otherwise, you have to pay the family forever."

Perched in a position that provides her with a view of Vallarta that most expats don't have, Allyna keeps a watchful eye on local politicians and their effect on the city she loves. "I'm not blind to the local political shenanigans, even though I can't report much of it because of the editorial thrust of the paper," she laments. "I've spoken with many people born and raised in Vallarta, and they tell me that there has never been anything as corrupt as the previous city administration, which thankfully left office at the end of 2006. They allegedly issued 167 building permits in the last fifteen days of that administration, which has resulted in the enormous number of real estate projects in the local construction pipeline. Many of those permits have been challenged and currently are in litigation. It's a disgrace."

Allyna is also unhappy with the disappearance of green spaces in Vallarta. "The three downtown parks—the only green areas outside of the Cuale River Island—were converted into parking lots to help alleviate the downtown parking problem. Two are underground, and the city has rebuilt parks on the ground level of the two structures. The major multistory garage on the Malecon, however, eliminated a park and provided no replacement. The amount of concrete in this city has driven the temperature of the downtown area up three degrees, and the dust everywhere has increased markedly. Another major environmental concern now facing this town is the preservation of the beautiful mountainsides that attracted so many of us to Vallarta in the first place. Every year they build on new sections of the mountainside. We have to start getting serious about our environment, or we're going to lose our little paradise."

Allyna is adamant that Vallarta's quality of life and the environment will not improve significantly until laws are properly implemented and enforced. "I have seen so many reports and plans to improve the local environment," she says. "One was an inch thick. But so few things ever get implemented. Planning is great, but action is a whole lot better. I go back to one of the basics I've been harping on for many years. The first thing the city can do to improve the environment is reduce the number of buses on the city streets. Every once in a while, we do a little survey at the *Vallarta Tribune*. We stand on a corner downtown and count the number of buses passing by in an hour. At one point we counted 157 buses in one hour, and most of them were nearly empty. They are big polluters because they are old buses. Unfortunately, I'm not very confident that much will happen because the unions are so strong."

She hasn't given up hope, though, for her jewel of the Mexican Riviera. "I hope fervently for an honest administration that will actually implement some of the excellent plans they have been developing over the years. The operative word here is implement. And enforce. I don't want to lose these beautiful mountains and the pristine bay that brought me here in the first place. And neither does anyone else. It is up to the city and the state to develop this area responsibly. I have my fingers crossed that they are up to the task."

CHAPTER FOURTEEN

HARRIET COCHRAN MURRAY

Divorced
Dallas, Texas
Owner/Operator, Cochran Murray Real Estate

"One of the hardest things we do in real estate is help
people who are moving here understand where they
are. They are living in Mexico where the culture, laws,
language, and most everything else is different."

A long-time Puerto Vallarta real estate professional, sixty-
five-year-old Harriet has her fingers on the pulse of current and
future real estate trends as the head of her own firm, Cochran
Murray Real Estate. She also writes a monthly real estate column for the popular monthly online publication pvmirror.com
and is an associate member of the Association of Mexican Real
Estate Professionals (AMPI).

Harriet's journey to paradise began in her hometown of
Monroe, Louisiana. She graduated from Northeast Louisiana
State University in Monroe with a degree in art education. Following graduation, she moved to New Orleans and taught art
in the public school system for a few years before moving to
Dallas, Texas, where she worked in the real estate business for
twenty-one years.

Before making her move to Puerto Vallarta full time, Harriet stayed at the well-known Ochos Cascadas condominium in the Conchas Chinas neighborhood, where she owned a time-share for many years. She had been vacationing in Vallarta since 1975, loved the place, but had no idea what it would be like to live in PV. She got her chance to find out in 1996, following a bad year for real estate in Texas. Harriet was invited by friends to stay with them in Vallarta for a longer period of time to learn what it would be like to live in another country. The choice wasn't difficult for beach-loving Harriet. She had always thought PV was one of the easiest places in Mexico to live because English was widely spoken and Vallarta had an international resort's social infrastructure.

Harriet hadn't planned to stay in Puerto Vallarta; she was just looking for a nice break from her real estate business in Texas. But after four months of living in paradise, she got restless and set out to find a job in PV. Leveraging her years of real estate experience, she took a job in time-share with the Westin hotel. She didn't do well in the time-share business because she found it so different from real estate and was fired four times before she finally threw in the towel after four months of trying.

Friends then encouraged her to start her own real estate business, which she did in 1997 after cutting her teeth with a local real estate firm. Cochran Murray Real Estate began with a focus only on buyers and their needs, similar to the business model she used in Texas. Her business started with one other person and now has grown to include Harriet, five agents, and a property management division.

Harriet's first six months in business were difficult as she immersed herself in the local real estate market and began to learn how to live and conduct business in Mexico. Unlike retirees, Harriet had to learn things much faster to survive. She believes that those who live here for six months out of the year don't really know what it is like to live in Vallarta on a day-to-day basis. "There's a whole business side to living here that is very different from being on vacation," Harriet notes. "When you have to go to five different offices to accomplish one task, like paying a bill, you begin to understand what it is like to live here full time."

Even with some difficulties making the transition to living in a foreign country, Harriet discovered that she had entered the local real estate market at just the right time. "From 1997 until 2005, real estate prices increased at approximately 10 percent a year and then accelerated to 20 percent a year for the last several years," Harriet recounts. "The market has been very strong and has continued at a fast pace because this is primarily a cash market that doesn't really depend upon financing. PV is not a credit market. Less than 10 percent of homes purchased here are financed. With baby boomers retiring, this could change as part of the overall mix, though. Financing has only been available for the past several years in Vallarta and has had some problems getting established. Part of the problem is that the market was initially flooded with lending companies, but their capability varied and now there is a shakeout going on. Additionally, most of the agents in Vallarta were not trained to handle financing."

Harriet believes the greater problem is that agents don't need a license to sell real estate in Mexico and many don't receive training from their own companies. Adding the complexities of the financing option made things even more difficult for the industry. "Many agents are hired to act as front men down here, and their roles often are more about just client relations," Harriet remarks. "They are not allowed to write contracts or get them closed. The Mexican government's attitude toward this has been, 'If you take people's jobs away from them, that's a bad thing.' As a result, they have not wanted to license real estate in Mexico."

Harriet points out, however, that the one area of the real estate business in Mexico that is licensed is the notario business. Notarios are specialized attorneys who are peculiar to Mexico and very different from the rest of the world. The notario is appointed for life.

Licensed or not, local agents are having a hard time keeping up with the demand for real estate in the Puerto Vallarta area. "Our local topography is enabling the growth of this area, particularly outside of Puerto Vallarta and along the Riviera Nayarit," Harriet explains. "All of the little inlets along the Pacific coast with their small, quaint villages are attracting developers because the inlets help protect the properties from the direct force of the ocean. Plus, the little villages all have their own restaurants and other services, and, importantly, buyers pay just a fraction of the cost they would pay in more developed areas like Vallarta. The idea is not to use PV as the anchor any longer, and frankly it can't continue to do it for that much longer anyway. Puerto Vallarta is up against the mountains and can only expand so much. It has geographical limitations. The same applies to the coast immediately south of PV, where the mountainous topography and available land to build on is limited. That is, until they finish the new highway to the south that will open up the Costa Allegre."

Harriet firmly believes that finding out what the buyer is really looking for and fitting the right property and location to the buyer's needs is the essence of her job as a real estate professional. "People in Bucerias wouldn't live in Vallarta; you couldn't give it to them," she says. "You have to first find out what people think they want and then decide where they really will fit." Bucerias—a thirty-minute drive up the north shore of the bay from PV—has its own center of activity within a six-block range where expats can enjoy their own restaurants, nightlife, and music. "They really don't want to drive in to Vallarta except once in a while," Harriet continues. "I started noticing this several years ago. People would get off the plane and be asked: 'Puerto Vallarta or Punta de Mita?' This was after all of the promotion Punta de Mita had done. It's more about the regional area now and not just Puerto Vallarta."

With more and more buyers looking at the entire region and not just the city of Puerto Vallarta, Harriet cautions that the area is generally not a playground for average income people. "Housing is not inexpensive here. Remember, this is still mainly a second home market for Americans and Canadians, where over 90 percent of the purchases are made with cash. By the way, we have found that the purchase profile of the Canadian buyer is somewhat different than the American. Canadians are much more conservative. They are not used to higher leveraged deals, so when they look at something, they don't buy emotionally. It has to have value. They are comparison shoppers. Americans tend to buy more on emotion. The local housing market overall, though, provides excellent investment opportunities for those who have the money to buy. Properties here hold their value over the long run. The fact that our weather is so great all the time and we live on a very large, protected bay are big plus factors. We just don't get the bad weather that Florida, the Caribbean, and other similar places get."

Harriet remembers that a few years ago AMPI—the local real estate association—conducted market research on the Puerto Vallarta area and found that the highest percentage of homeowners were from New York. The West Coast of the U.S. was second and Chicago third. "We also found out that people who bought here had vacationed in PV an average of six times and had purchased because they had a friend who had already bought here," Harriet recalls. "They often begin by purchasing a time-share and then move up to a condo or a house. House owners, if they stay here long enough, then downsize from a house to a condo."

Most expats own homes, but renting is an option, even though finding a long-term, reasonably priced rental in a resort area is a more difficult proposition. "It has always been a market more focused on short-term rentals to tourists, which naturally makes all properties more expensive," Harriet says. "It makes sense that people who own properties here primarily to rent them out can make much more money from short-term rentals. Those who want a long-term rental find they must network as much as possible to find available opportunities. Often, renters must move three or four times before they find just the right place. All of the normal renting restrictions apply down here, also. Condominiums generally don't allow pets, and many homes restrict pets, also."

Purchasing that dream home in paradise is just the beginning of an adventure that also can bring frustrations and challenges, Harriet thinks. "One of the hardest things we do in real estate is help people who are moving here understand where they are. They are living in Mexico where the culture, laws, language, and most everything else is different. To be successful in living here, they need to understand and learn. The best way to explain it is to tell them to 'locate yourself.' Don't be judgmental, and remember where you are. Things operate down here the way Mexicans want them to; if they didn't want them to operate this way, they would change the laws, the customs, and their way of life. They need to understand that Mexicans are much more independent than Americans or Canadians. Mexicans do not like to be told what to do. They are so independent that they only depend upon themselves, their families, and their best friends. If you live here, you will have to acquire the tools of how to operate in Mexico. You can't just say: 'We don't do this in New York or in L.A.' You have to adapt to living in Mexico."

Harriet offers some final advice for Americans and Canadians thinking of moving to Puerto Vallarta: "Don't move down here just because you think you're going to save on the cost of living. Living can be on any level you want, but replicating your current lifestyle at a much lower cost is really not that feasible any longer. If you want your piece of paradise on a lower budget, you'll probably have to go to those areas much farther out of town where property is less expensive and services are far fewer."

CHAPTER FIFTEEN

PAM THOMPSON

Divorced
Visalia, California
Owner/Operator, Health Care Resources
Puerto Vallarta

"Americans always want to know when we will get
Medicare coverage in Mexico. My answer is probably
not in my lifetime."

No one knows more about health care needs and resources
in Puerto Vallarta than California baby boomer Pam Thompson. And few people are as well-connected and know the community better than Pam. In fact, it would be very safe to say
that for expats who live in Vallarta or tourists who vacation
here, Pam is unquestionably the go-to person if you need help
finding medical assistance.

This doyenne of Vallarta's health care world grew up in the
center of California where she went to Fresno State University
and became a nurse, following in the footsteps of other family
members who worked in the medical profession. After graduation, Pam worked for a large California regional hospital in
Visalia, where her family had worked for a combined total of
some two hundred years.

Her first taste of Vallarta was in the mid-1980s when she and her twenty-something friends first arrived on the local scene. It was Pam's first trip to Mexico. Pam loved the weather, the people, the beach, and the mountains so much she started coming often and alone, which she preferred. Because of her work schedule, she could come only every six months, although she wanted to be here even more frequently.

While on vacation in Vallarta, she made friends with several Mexican families, whom she stayed in touch with and saw each time she visited. "It made my trips to Vallarta so much more satisfying," Pam remembers. "Having good friends to see and that connection with the local people made such a great difference."

Her life began to change when her former husband moved to Oregon to take a new job and Pam's son decided to go with him. Now that her son wanted to live with his dad, Pam no longer was tied to California and started thinking seriously about fulfilling her dream to live in Puerto Vallarta. She accelerated her trips south but found that it became more and more difficult to return home after each trip. "I just wanted to do something else. Visalia was very family-oriented, and I couldn't see myself living there in twenty years."

Pam admits that she is a very cautious person who likes to think things through, so it took her a long time to make the final decision to move to Vallarta. Her decision-making process was helped along while visiting PV in 1988. She spoke with a woman who had a laboratory and a clinic and was interested in starting prenatal Lamaze classes. It sounded like a perfect way to relocate to Vallarta and use her experience and skill set. She agreed to make the move, but the job didn't pan out, and Pam found herself looking for work. A good planner, she had set aside money to live on for some time, which allowed her enough time to find a new job.

She was fortunate to find a job as a local rep for a Canadian tour operator for her first five years living in Vallarta. The job provided her with an opportunity to really get to know the city, especially the tourism industry. She enjoyed working in that industry but felt that being a part of a smaller operation might fit her needs better. She left her tour operator job for a much smaller company that ran day cruises on the bay. "The job was probably the biggest challenge of my life," Pam sighs. "But, we turned the company around, and now it is doing well."

After the ups and downs of the tourism business, Pam decided in 2001 to go back to her roots in the medical field. She started working for Global as a coordinator for both the ground and air ambulance services the company provided. While she was working at Global, Cornerstone Hospital was being planned, and Pam was asked to help with that process. She tried to do both jobs, but it became too much, so she left Global to focus exclusively on her Cornerstone work. She became the hospital's international services and patient coordinator when Cornerstone opened its doors. The hospital job became an excellent platform for the formation of Health Care Resources Puerto Vallarta, a business Pam started in 2007.

Her timing was perfect. "The market was really ripe for my services," Pam recounts. "The medical infrastructure began improving significantly with the construction of San Javier Hospital in 2001, which is located across from the cruise ship terminal. Several other smaller hospitals existed before San Javier opened, but the new hospital changed the playing field with its state-of-the-art medical technology. The other major change that occurred to significantly improve health delivery services in Vallarta was the influx of physicians with specialty expertise. With the rapid growth of the city, the increase in tourism, and the opening of hospitals with advanced technology, specialists from all over Mexico began moving to PV, most bilingual. Vallarta now has cardiac specialists who perform bypass surgery, negating the need to have the procedure done in Guadalajara or other major cities within Mexico. Hospital emergency rooms, also, are equal to most trauma centers in the U.S. and Canada, and there are several twenty-four-hour ambulance services with well-trained paramedics and air ambulance service, if required."

Pam points with pride to Puerto Vallarta's five state-of-the-art health care facilities that meet or exceed U.S. standards and offer MRI, CAT scan, dialysis, and other modern technology. "The two best-equipped hospitals in Puerto Vallarta today are San Javier and Cornerstone, but the new competition has spurred remodeling projects by the older city hospitals. Several major diagnostic centers also have been built to support the hospital growth, most of them with advanced technology. The local health care facilities can handle most major illnesses with a few exceptions. Radiation and chemotherapy treatment, for example, has to be done in either Tepic, Nayarit, or in Guadalajara, although once on chemotherapy most of the treatment can be done locally, if the patient chooses. Our dream is to have a cancer center located in Vallarta."

Another specialist Pam says is missing from the local health care offering is a rheumatologist, which she finds amazing considering the number of retired people who live in Vallarta. Patients must travel to Guadalajara for that treatment, as well as laser eye surgery. And, although laboratories are plentiful in the area, there is no pathologist in Vallarta. All biopsies need to be sent to either Tepic or Guadalajara.

Even with the rapid improvement in top-quality medical care, prices remain comparatively low. "In general I would say that overall health care costs here are 40 percent less than the U.S.," Pam figures. "Although inpatient care costs at the local hospitals have gone up, they are still much less than the United

States. But for CAT scans, MRI, and other diagnostic work, as well as physician consultations, the costs are way, way less. Dental work, plastic surgery, and other surgical procedures also are significantly less. Because of the cost, we are seeing a growing business in what is called medical tourism. It's popular with many Canadians who often face long waits for medical procedures under their national health care plan. Interestingly, one of the most in-demand procedures tourists seek is bariatric surgery, also known as weight-loss surgery."

Although Pam's company opened for business just a year ago, it's already a very successful operation. The company offers multiple no-charge and minimal charge health care resources services to Vallarta residents and tourists alike, mostly English-speaking. "We're a one-stop resource for all your medical needs, including handling all of the paperwork," Pam says. "Our company provides assistance in finding the right physician to match the medical needs of the patient, including in-home and hotel visits or other emergency health needs. There are over a thousand physicians in Vallarta, but we work with just eighty in our referral program. We screen all of the physicians we recommend, including their bilingual capability. I'm very happy because we have been averaging about 140 scheduled appointments per month."

Pam provides an example of a typical referral they would handle. "A man called me from a yacht to say that he had a medical problem, did not speak Spanish, and needed to see someone right away. We got his background over the phone and were able to match him up with a certified physician who could see him right away. After the appointment, we followed up with the patient to ensure that he was satisfied. Patients, by the way, are not charged for any of these services."

Importantly, Pam's company handles all of the necessary paperwork, including health insurance claims. They prepare, translate, and submit claims to insurance companies, which can be quite an ordeal in Mexico. The multi-faceted services extend also to home care, which was not readily available before she started her company. They provide nurses and aides for both short-term and long-term care.

Pam's company also fills a void that has always existed in Puerto Vallarta. On a regular basis, the company holds clinics for a variety of medical needs. A mammogram clinic, for example, is held every two months. For about seventy dollars, those attending the clinic receive a mammogram, an examination by an oncologist, and an educational program. Pam's company also offers an ongoing speakers program on a wide variety of topics, access to support groups, and the latest health information and news.

She is also capitalizing on the new, rapidly growing medical tourism segment of the health care industry. "We are seeing increasing demand for dental surgery, plastic surgery, hip replacements, eye surgery, and other popular procedures. Vallarta is a great vacation destination, and when people begin finding out about the quality of the medical care we have here and the capability of our physicians, medical tourism is going to grow by leaps and bounds. The impetus for Americans is certainly going to be cost and for Canadians, being able to get a procedure done on vacation while not having to wait months for an appointment."

This year Pam's company will introduce a membership card. For around thirty dollars a year, card holders will receive a plastic photo ID card that will contain pertinent medical information and will allow the holder to receive discounts at labs and other health services. Detailed medical information will be taken as part of the card application process, including end-of-life wishes, blood type, and preferences. This information will be kept in a file and matched to the patient's card number. The card will also provide no-fee access to many of the events and programs conducted by the company throughout the year and a list of key emergency telephone numbers.

Pam's company also offers a choice of ten different international and Mexican health insurance companies to choose from—including the health services arm of Mexican Social Security (IMSS)—and will help you select your best option. International or Mexican plans are the best option for expats and are significantly lower in price than health insurance plans purchased in the U.S. Medicare, however, is not available to Americans living in Mexico. "Americans always want to know when we will get Medicare coverage in Mexico," Pam sighs. "My answer is probably not in my lifetime."

Pam is fifty-two, so Medicare coverage in Mexico will not happen for a very long time. However, she points out that Medicare supplemental insurance—although not accepted in Mexico—can be used in Puerto Vallarta because the providers will reimburse the expenses. "It doesn't matter what kind of insurance you have. For outpatient services, x-rays, consultation, and many other services, you have to pay out-of-pocket and send in the paperwork for reimbursement. But for inpatient services, most of the major hospitals are contracted with a wide range of health insurance providers, although you still have to use a credit card for a deposit, usually up to about a thousand dollars. Companies also will reimburse for emergency services, supplemental to Medicare.

Pam offers a few pointers to help navigate the health care system in Mexico. "First, never pay a bill until you get a receipt. Second, register with your consulate when you arrive. Third, have end-of-life and do-not-resuscitate documents drawn in Vallarta, since Mexican law does not recognize living wills. My company has a program that utilizes a bilingual attorney to draw up a Mexican will, which will then be kept on file with the appropriate local consulate."

Looking to what the future holds for health care services, Pam believes that within five years medical tourism will be a major part of the local economy. "It's a win/win situation for everybody. Both the tourism and medical industries will benefit from this development, as long as people don't get greedy. Vallarta has the potential to become a major medical tourism destination."

She also believes Vallarta is ripe for the development of the same kind of assisted living facilities that are found in other retirement areas. "They haven't existed yet primarily because Mexican families culturally and historically have taken care of their elders. But, the full-time, year-round American and Canadian retiree population is growing and will in the near future be able to sustain those kinds of facilities."

Improving the long-term quality of life in Vallarta is uppermost in Pam's mind. She thinks the city and the people of Vallarta need to do a whole lot more to protect the environment, which has a direct bearing on long-term health concerns. Pam's son moved to Puerto Vallarta to be near his mom, married, and is now raising a family here. "I have grandchildren who live in PV and know there is nowhere to take them, other than the beach. Vallarta is devoid of open green spaces, other than the sports field across from the Sheraton hotel. There also are no public swimming pools for them to use. Many other cities in Mexico have paid attention to the recreational needs of their citizens, but Vallarta has depended upon the bountiful blessings of the bay for too many years. We have increased traffic and air pollution, too much concrete, and not enough green spaces. All this adds up to a future of more health concerns. Thankfully, the local health community is growing and improving and is up to the challenge."

CHAPTER SIXTEEN

VALLARTA MAÑANA

Will paradise be lost? What will Puerto Vallarta look like in ten years? The directors of tourism for both the city of Puerto Vallarta and the state of Jalisco have similar views of Vallarta's future. From their perspectives, paradise will remain, but it will be bigger and, hopefully, better.

Marcelo Alcaráz offers the city of Puerto Vallarta's vision of the future as its director of tourism, serving under the current city mayor, Javier Bravo. The Bravo administration took office in January 2007, almost concurrent with the start of the new state of Jalisco government. Sr. Alcaráz believes that the Guadalajara-based state government is extremely interested in Puerto Vallarta because it considers the city its "crown jewel" of tourism. The state of Jalisco's Director of Tourism José Estrada—who is based in Puerto Vallarta—agrees with his counterpart and confirms state plans to provide the necessary funds to burnish the luster of its "crown jewel."

According to Puerto Vallarta's Sr. Alcaráz, one of the immediate problems the city government has tackled is the growing traffic problem, particularly in the downtown area. He says the main problem is the thirty-two different bus routes that serve the city center. Alcaráz thinks there should be a maximum of eight routes and that reducing the number of buses would have a major impact on reducing traffic congestion. Currently, the city is negotiating with the three bus unions. "As a first step to relieving traffic congestion, the city and the bus unions are working together to reach an agreement on reducing the number of bus routes into the city," Alcaráz explains. "Those discussions are ongoing, but no agreement has been reached yet."

Farther off and in the conceptual stage at this time is a transfer center for all city buses. As a second step to relieving traffic congestion, Puerto Vallarta would like to build a large garage that could be used for bus transfers and as a public parking structure. Sr. Alcaráz believes that the sports center across from the Sheraton hotel on the near north side of Puerto Vallarta would make an ideal location for building a subterranean structure under the sports field. Other locations are also being discussed, but the cost of the project is a major timing factor. If built, only a few buses would be authorized to operate in the downtown area, and they would be modern "eco buses" with air conditioning, accommodations for the disabled as well as bike riders, and have other modern features.

The transit center would also include additional parking for cars so drivers could park in the facility and then transfer to buses to go into town. The additional parking in the transit center would help alleviate the parking problems that now exist in the city's core. Puerto Vallarta is asking the federal government in Mexico City to participate in the funding along with the state of Jalisco. Sr. Alcaráz says the goal is to first develop a specific plan of action and then begin implementing that plan within the next four years before the current state government leaves office.

In addition to transit planning, Puerto Vallarta also is building new streets and expanding existing ones that parallel the main thoroughfare from the international airport to downtown. For example, the upgrading of the existing Avenida Federacion—a north-south highway that provides a connection to the Vista Vallarta golf course—to four lanes and connecting it to the main thoroughfare of Avenida Francisco Villa is underway. This new construction should help the north-to-south traffic flow into the city center. Also, part of this construction project is the building of additional bridges to connect existing roads.

Another welcome addition to the local highway infrastructure is the addition of a second tunnel that will improve traffic flow on Avenida Libramiento, currently the only city bypass avenue. Vallarta's Sr. Alcaráz reports that construction has begun, and the project will be completed within the next several years. The new bore will be for northbound traffic and will be located a little east of the existing tunnel.

Both directors of tourism point to other new highway projects on the immediate horizon that should significantly relieve local traffic congestion. A contract for the new Puerto Vallarta bypass highway will be let in 2008 and will take approximately three years to complete. Jalisco's Sr. Estrada notes that the project will connect the town of Las Palmas north of the airport to Boca de Tomatlan, approximately ten miles south of Puerto Vallarta. He calls the new four-lane highway a "macro Libramiento," because it will provide a modern highway around the city for vehicles—especially buses and trucks—to completely bypass city traffic.

Sr. Estrada outlines other major highway improvements either in the pipeline or coming soon. The federal government has a mandate from Mexico's President Calderon to significantly improve the country's infrastructure. To that end, work has begun on a new highway from the Guadalajara area to the state of Nayarit's coast that will shave an hour or more off the driving time between Guadalajara and Puerto Vallarta. The new highway will cut across the mountains from the town of Jale on the existing Mexican federal Highway 15 to the west coast town of Puerta de Lima and then head south to Bucerias on the

Bay of Banderas' north shore. To better connect with the new Vallarta bypass highway, the existing road between Bucerias and Las Palmas will also be upgraded to accommodate a much heavier traffic flow.

Access to and from the coast south of Puerto Vallarta is also scheduled for a big improvement, according to the state's Sr. Estrada. A new four-lane coastal highway will connect Manzanillo in the south to the southern terminus of the Vallarta bypass highway in Boca de Tomatlan. The new highway is designed to spur low-density development of Jalisco's Costa Allegre and provide better access to the major cities of Manzanillo and Puerto Vallarta. The new highway will also link to the new international airport being built by the state in Tomatlan. The airport—named Campo Acosta—has been designed initially to handle jets with up to a hundred-passenger capacity and open the Costa Allegre to major tourism. As the area develops, the airport will be expanded to accommodate growth.

Both tourism directors also are excited by the possibility of water taxis as a piece of the long-range traffic solution for the Bay of Banderas. The city and representatives from the state government in Guadalajara will discuss the new transportation potential with officials from Vancouver, British Columbia, a city well known for its water taxi system. The project would involve the entire bay, not just the state of Jalisco. The state's Sr. Estrada visualizes new piers at Nuevo Vallarta, Los Muertos beach, La Cruz de Huanacaxtle, the PV Malecon, and Marina Vallarta. He hopes that by 2009 a water taxi is operating between Nuevo Vallarta and Puerto Vallarta's downtown Malecon.

Many of the infrastructure improvements now being implemented, planned, or imagined have been designed to improve the local environment. Puerto Vallarta Mayor Bravo ran for office partially on a "green" platform and appears to be working toward that end. His tourism director confirms that the city is focusing on environmental improvements to protect the city's future. In late 2007, the city began implementing a federal program to ensure that air, water, and other environmental standards will be met by Puerto Vallarta, in compliance with a global environmental agreement signed by Mexico and ninety-nine other countries in Brazil. The agreement calls for all countries to comply with basic environmental guidelines. To begin that process, two years ago Mexican government environmental experts conducted a thorough analysis of the local environment and established specific benchmarks for the area. Actual monitoring of benchmark achievements will be done through a global organization called Green Globe, which monitors the progress each country is making in meeting the guidelines spelled out in the Brazil agreement.

Vallarta's Sr. Alcaráz says the city has just started work on programs to comply with the agreement. For example, a new city dump is being built as part of a new recycling program that has just been introduced. Homeowners and businesses must now separate their trash for pick up. City trucks eventually will haul the trash to a planned new recycling facility that will process trash that can then be recycled, with the balance going to the new city dump.

To ensure compliance with the environmental agreement, Puerto Vallarta has implemented two important programs: Clean Vallarta and Children's Clean Vallarta Club. Clean Vallarta was designed to develop community awareness for keeping the city clean. Children's Clean Vallarta Club turns kids into clean city promoters. They are taught the benefits of recycling at their schools with the hope that they in turn will educate their parents to keep trash separated and keep the city clean.

The city also has launched a school educational program in the small cities that ring the Jalisco side of the bay. The program educates students on the impact of stream pollution on the bay and instills in them a sense of pride and environmental stewardship. To ensure clean bay water, the city is also building new sewage treatment plants. Two are currently in service, two—in Boca de Tomatlan and Las Palmas—are brand new and not yet working, and another in Mismaloya is in the process of development.

Sr. Alcaráz thinks, however, that the most important development for Puerto Vallarta is the updating of the urban plan for the city. He notes that the plan provides an integral model of community development, which includes the primary zoning of land use, the reorganization of the city into districts, and a traffic system in accordance with the future growth of Puerto Vallarta, among other things. The document must first be authorized by the city council and then presented to the public, where comments on the proposals will be received.

The planning process also takes crime into consideration, which is always foremost in the minds of those who live in Puerto Vallarta as well as those thinking of moving to the city. Sr. Alcaráz believes Puerto Vallarta is the safest tourist destination by comparison with similar resorts in Mexico. He says Vallarta is fortunate that the drug syndicates have not focused their activity on Puerto Vallarta at this time, although several recent killings in the city have been linked to drug crimes, and the military has moved in to establish drug search checkpoints north and south of the city. Crime statistics provided by the administration are categorized as misdemeanor, civil court, and federal court actions. Misdemeanors represent the bulk of the crime, representing nearly 60 percent of the total in 2007. Civil court action, which encompasses more serious crimes like murder, was nearly 30 percent of the total, and federal court activity represented the balance. The biggest change in crime activity over the last five years has been an increase in civil court crimes, which have climbed from around 23 percent of the total from 2002 through 2005 to just over 29 percent in both 2006 and 2007, reflective to a degree of mounting drug-related activity and the city's booming growth.

The management of the area's growth is of equal concern to both directors of tourism. Puerto Vallarta's Sr. Alcaráz projects that most of the growth will occur in the neighboring state of Nayarit and the area south of Cabo Corrientes, the southern tip of the bay. The state of Nayarit is planning for nearly one million people by the year 2012 in the Riviera Nayarit arc, which extends from Nuevo Vallarta to San Blas, a coastal city west of the state capitol of Tepic. He believes the area south of the bay, with the addition of the new international airport along the Costa Allegre and the construction of new highways that will provide access to the beaches, will boom over the next ten years.

Sr. Alcaráz also maintains that Vallarta will stay focused on preserving the old colonial charm that the city is well known for and improving its infrastructure, rather than promoting continued growth. In 2007, PV began investing ten million dollars in a downtown facelift. City crews have been busy on a number of projects such as putting all utility lines underground, reconstructing the charming cobblestone streets, and repainting building facades to continue the whitewashed look with red tile roofs, a signature visual characteristic of Puerto Vallarta. Neon signs have been taken down, also, and store signs must now meet specific aesthetic guidelines.

The city also is tackling its growth problems to improve the quality of life for both its flourishing tourist trade and its citizens. The future will be less core city growth, a better physical infrastructure, environmental improvements, and speedier ways to get around the city. "We want to preserve our 'crown jewel,'" says Sr. Alcaráz, "for not only the millions of tourists who have enjoyed and will enjoy our city, but importantly for those who call this beautiful city their home."

The state's vision of Vallarta's future is similar but more expansive, with development of the Costa Allegre of equal importance to protecting the "crown jewel." To further this vision of the future, both federal and state governments recently opened offices in Puerto Vallarta to help ensure that municipalities around the bay respect their original development plans and implement them properly. Jalisco's Sr. Estrada articulates the need for future growth with order and foresees environmental concerns playing an even greater role in the further development of the area.

"As the coast south of the Bay of Banderas is developed," Sr. Estrada explains, "we will be applying tight controls and regulation for development. We want to ensure that there will be low impact on the environment." The highway and airport infrastructure improvements are essential to sound growth, he believes.

Ten years from now, the state's Sr. Estrada sees Puerto Vallarta as a larger city well connected to both the north and south and serving as a modern service center for more far flung communities on the coast and in the mountains. "The key is to have a master plan for all municipalities and ensure they are properly implemented," he says. "We can't stop the growth, but we can shape it in the best possible way."

Both directors offer sanguine predictions for PV, but as the past has shown all too often, the future does not always unfold as intended. Both city and state governments should be applauded for their new devotion to long-term planning in the wake of the area's explosive growth, but their commitment to orderly growth will be tested during the implementation phase. Getting the local bus unions to agree on anything, for example, is an old story that seems to have no ending. Local expats have heard it before, but continue to hope for the best.

Baby boomers—many who sank their roots in Vallarta many years ago—generally take the changes to their town in stride and see more good than bad. Bobbie Snyder sums up the feelings of most Vallarta boomers when she says earlier in Chapter Seven: "We're here for the duration, even with all of the growth and changes we have seen. The fact is that everybody comes here with the expectation that this is Mexico, but they want to change it to be like home. They want to bring certain things with them so that life is easier and more familiar for them. In many respects, Vallarta is becoming more and more like the States or Canada, with Home Depot, Sam's, Wal-Mart, Costco, and the enclosed malls. It didn't exist before, and that's why people would come here. That's a big reason why we came here. Now, they could be anywhere. It's a big international resort city, not the charming, small town we once knew. I don't think it's necessarily a negative, it's just what happens when growth comes to stay."

And stay it surely will. The boomer wave is coming to Mexico, ready or not, and will continue for a long time. If you're flexible, adventurous, a risk taker, and can take growth and new life experiences in stride like Bobbie and her boomer peers in PV, this paradise may indeed be the place for you.

ABOUT THE AUTHOR

Puerto Vallarta-based writer Robert Nelson has lived in the Mexican tropical paradise for six years. He has closely observed the baby boomer generation during his nearly forty-year professional career, working in radio, advertising, public relations, marketing, and brand consulting prior to beginning his full-time writing career. As a brand consultant in the San Francisco Bay Area and in Puerto Vallarta, he worked with major global brands like Driscoll's Strawberries and Expedia. He also was an adjunct professor of advertising at San Jose State University, where he received his master's of science degree in mass communications. More information about the author and his work can be found at his Web site: http://www.robertnelsonwriter.com.

Well-known Puerto Vallarta artist Ada Colorina provided the colorful art for this book. Ms. Colorina's style is generally categorized as "naïve" or "primitive" in the tradition of the great Mexican artist Manuel Lepe. You can find out more about Ada Colorina and her work at her Web site: http://www.adacolorina.com.

SOURCES

Agren, David. "Foreigners Invade Jalisco." http://www.agren.blogspot (accessed January 26, 2008).

"Baby Boomer." *Wikipedia.* http://www.en.wikipedia.org/wiki/Baby_boomer (accessed January 7, 2008).

"Baby Boomers Swell Ranks of Retirement-Aged Canadians." *CBC News.* (July 17, 2007) http://www.cbc.ca/canada/story/2007/07/17/census-canada.html (accessed January 16, 2008).

"Boom in Mexico Real Estate for Baby Boomers and Retirees." http://www.thematuremarket.com (accessed January 7, 2008).

Butler, Jim. "Mexico Gets Hotter As Baby Boomers Approach Retirement." http://*hotellaw.jmbm.com*/2006/10/hospitality_lawyer_mexico_gets.html (accessed January 7, 2008).

Camhi, Dee Dee. Personal interview. Recorded March 11, 2008.

Davis, Mike. "Gringos Turn Tide Crossing Border." *San Francisco Chronicle* (October 15, 2006). http://www.*sfgate.com* (accessed January 7, 2008).

Metlife Mature Market Institute. *The Metlife Survey of American Attitudes Toward Retirement: What's Changed.* October, 2005.

Metlife Mature Market Institute. *Boomers: Ready to Launch Study*. November, 2007 Highlights.

"Oldest Baby Boomers Turn 60." January 3, 2006. http://www.*census.gov* (accessed January 7, 2008).

Sheridan, Laura. "The World's Top Retirement Havens in 2007." *International Living* (September 1, 2007). http://www.internationalliving.com (accessed April 17, 2008).

Thompson, Adam. "Surging Market Attracts Baby Boomers." *Financial Times* (November 19, 2007). http://www.ft.com (accessed January 7, 2008).

Vann, Korky. "Boomers' Fashion A New Model For Retirement." *The Hartford Courant* (April 16, 2008). http://www.courant.com (accessed April 16, 2008).

Youden, John. "Puerto Vallarta: A Real Estate Success Story." *The Real Estate Guide*. April 2008: 42 – 46.

Zuckerman, Sam. "Retirement Money Worries Mount for Workers." *San Francisco Chronicle* (May 20, 2008). http://www.sfgate.com (accessed May 20, 2008).

41067431R10099

Made in the USA
San Bernardino, CA
06 November 2016